Understanding Financial Accounts

If you want to know how . . .

Cash Flows and Budgeting Made Easy
How to set and monitor financial targets in any organisation

Make Marketing Work for You
How to use proven marketing techniques to your own advantage

Financing a New Business
How to raise the funds to set up your own successful business

Starting Your Own Business
How to plan, build and manage a successful enterprise

Mastering Book-Keeping
A step-by-step guide to the principles and practice of business accounting

Preparing a Winning Business Plan
How to plan to succeed and secure financial backing

howtobooks

For full details, please send for a free copy of the
latest catalogue to:
How To Books
3 Newtec Place, Magdalen Road
Oxford OX4 1RE, United Kingdom
info@howtobooks.co.uk
www.howtobooks.co.uk

Understanding Financial Accounts

Understanding the principles and practice of accounting – from book-keeping to VAT

Second edition

PHIL STONE

howtobooks

Published by How To Books Ltd
3 Newtec Place, Magdalen Road
Oxford, OX4 1RE, United Kingdom
Tel: (01865) 793806. Fax: (01865) 248780
email: info@howtobooks.co.uk
www.howtobooks.co.uk

First published 2001
Second edition 2003

British Library Cataloguing in Publication Data
A catalogue record for this book is available from the British
Library

Cover design by Baseline Arts Ltd, Oxford

Produced for How To Books by Deer Park Productions.
Typeset by TW Typesetting, Plymouth, Devon
Printed and bound by Cromwell Press, Trowbridge, Wiltshire

NOTE: The material contained in this book is set out in good
faith for general guidance and no liability can be accepted for
loss or expense incurred as a result of relying in particular
circumstances on statements made in this book. Laws and
regulations may be complex and liable to change, and readers
should check the current position with the relevant
authorities before making personal arrangements.

Contents

List of Illustrations

Preface

Being able to use accounting in your business does not require years of training. Having said that, I am not suggesting that you can replace the services of your accountant. Your accountant is there to provide specialist help and guidance. This will not, however, be forthcoming on a daily basis unless you can afford to pay them for such involvement.

By understanding the techniques of accounting in your business you can use accounting to control your business more effectively. By using the advice in this book you will be able to take practical control of the day to day financial side of running your business. Not only should this make you more efficient, it will also help your bank and your accountant.

By showing your bank that you have control over your finances they may be more willing to support you if you need to borrow money. By keeping your records in a proper format you will help your accountant to prepare your final accounts. In real terms this should save you money.

Small business accounting is all about being practical. It is not difficult and once you understand the rules it should all fall into place. Maintaining tight control of your finances is essential if your business is to succeed. By tracking your finances you should be able to see problems before they occur. This does, at the very least, give you time to put them right.

Phil Stone MBA, Dip M, Dip FS, ACIB

(1)

Understanding the Basic Principles

The accountancy profession has a number of rules relating to the preparation of financial accounts. These are the Statements of Standard Accounting Practice, SSAPs for short. For all practical purposes you do not need to understand these. As a business owner you can leave them to your accountant and they can advise you if any are relevant to you, subsequently making the necessary adjustments in your final accounts.

The only principle that you need to be concerned with is accuracy. Your records must be accurate if you are to rely on them for management information. In many ways it will not matter which method of accounting you use. The important point to remember is that you must remain consistent in your method. Initially your accountant can help you with establishing your accounting records. It will make their and your lives a lot easier if you both use the same methods.

In this way you can probably also reduce the amount of work they undertake. This, of course, will ultimately have an effect on the fee that they charge.

- If you present them with a shoe box full of receipts and bank statements then you can expect to pay dearly for your final accounts.

- If, on the other hand, you present them with draft accounts it merely leaves them to check your figures and sign off the finished accounts.

DOUBLE ENTRY BOOK-KEEPING

There are a number of different methods you can use to keep your accounts. Whilst they are simple to use they do not allow for any real management information to be made available to you in a timely manner. This simplicity, despite being advantageous, also has disadvantages in maintaining control over your finances. From the outset I would strongly recommend that you use a full double entry book-keeping system.

A double entry system will entail more work for you but this extra effort will reap rewards in the future.

Control of your finances is crucial to your business and time spent on your accounts represents a good investment. Allocate time each day to look after your books and the task will become a lot easier. Leaving their preparation until the end of the week, or even worse, the end of the month, will mean a lot of additional work for you.

Understanding the two simple rules

As you would expect, double entry book-keeping involves making two entries in your records. The two simple rules in this respect are:

- ◆ debit the account of the receiver of value
- ◆ credit the account of the giver of that value.

At first sight this might seem to go against what you might have thought. For example, if you look at your bank statements your account, if a positive figure, is in credit. If overdrawn, or negative, it is in debit. If you reflect on this for a moment you will see that the bank is actually following the same rules:

- ◆ Your account is in credit because you have given the bank value. You are therefore a creditor.

- ◆ If in debit it is because you have received value and owe the bank money. In other words you are a debtor.

To give a practical example of the double entry system consider the following scenario.

Example
You start your business with an investment of £5,000 which is paid into the bank. In your accounting records you therefore debit £5,000 to the bank record and credit £5,000 to your capital account.

To help you run your business you then purchase a computer system from a retailer at a cost of £1,000. The entries for this are a debit for £1,000 to your equipment account and a corresponding credit to your bank account.

The difference between debtors and creditors
Using the double entry system means that you will have two different balances in your books:

◆ debtors on one side
◆ and creditors on the other.

It is usual for debit balances to be on the left of your books and credit balances on the right.

Having worked through the two simple rules of the double entry system it should be apparent that the figures in your books, representing debtors and creditors should balance. In other words both sides should be equal.

The reason for this is that the debtors represent your assets and the creditors represent your liabilities. Taking the example above, the £5,000 debit balance at the bank is money that you have, an asset. The capital account credit balance is money that is owed by the business, in this case to you as the investor. When you purchase the computer equipment the overall total balance of debtors and creditors remains the same. The only difference now is the accounts to which the balances are allocated. Summarising the accounts would give the balances shown in Figure 1.

Debtors		**Creditors**	
Bank	£4,000	Capital	£5,000
Equipment	£1,000		
Totals	£5,000		£5,000

Fig. 1. The double entry system.

The summarising of the accounts is looked at in greater detail later in this chapter when we consider the construction of a trial balance.

Allocating accounts

There are three types of account that you will use in your double entry system:

- personal accounts
- nominal accounts
- real accounts.

Personal accounts

Personal accounts are allocated to your debtors and creditors. They relate to the people that either owe you money or to whom you owe money. There is also one personal account that relates to your investment in your business, the capital account.

Nominal accounts

Nominal accounts are allocated for revenue and expenses. For example, rent and postage costs that relate to expenses and sales which relate to revenue. In all cases it is a record of either money paid or money received, but the actual cash has either been paid into, or out of, either the cash or bank account.

Real accounts

Real accounts are accounts that record the physical assets of the business. Because these are tangible assets they will always be debit balances and examples of such accounts include:

- land and buildings
- plant and machinery
- tools and equipment
- motor vehicles.

THE RECORDS YOU NEED

Exactly how you organise your financial records is up to you. You can operate a box-file system or you can purchase proper ledger books from a stationer. The important point is that you decide what it is you need from the outset. Unfortunately, many businesses start off with one system and upon realising that this will be inadequate, they are forced to make changes. This usually involves duplication of work which can be very time-consuming.

At this stage it is worth approaching your accountant for advice. They will have experience of other similar sized businesses and can advise on the most appropriate system for you.

> By working with your accountant to design your accounting system you will also make their life easier in the long-term.

This is even more important if you are considering computerising your accounting. It will make the transfer of information much easier if you are using software that is compatible with that used by your accountant.

The importance of documentation

Obviously proper records can only be kept with proper documentation. Every single payment that you make, and any money that you receive must be properly documented.

In terms of expenses you will require supporting receipts.

Where a receipt cannot be obtained for any reason then a petty cash voucher will need to be generated.

> Without exception, every item of expenditure must be covered by documentation recording the payment that has been made.

On the other side of the coin is your sales income. When you make a cash sale this should be recorded, usually by a till receipt. In terms of sales on credit, these will all be covered by an appropriate invoice.

Great care needs to be taken with your documentation. If you are VAT registered your books could be inspected by HM Customs and Excise at any time. The Inland Revenue will also need to be satisfied that the statements you make to them in your tax return are verifiable.

The importance of adequate documentation cannot be over emphasised. Make sure you have a piece of paper to support every single entry in your books.

The cash book
The cash book will combine your cash account and your bank account. As with all of the other books or ledgers mentioned in this chapter, an appropriate accounting book can be purchased from any good stationer. These will provide you with the appropriate columns in which to make the entries.

For the vast majority of businesses the cash book will involve the highest number of entries. This is because most payments or receipts will involve either a movement of cash or a payment from the bank account.

The sales ledger

As the name suggests, this will record all of your sales which might be cash sales or credit sales. Each time an invoice is raised it will be recorded in the sales ledger. When the invoice is paid it will be marked accordingly. Outstanding invoices, or the debtor total, can be checked each month and chased for payment if necessary. Payments received for the month can also be compared with the cash book.

The purchases ledger

The purchases ledger works in the same way as the sales ledger although it obviously records all purchases. As an invoice is received it will be entered in the ledger and then annotated when paid. Each month the invoices that have been paid should be compared with the cash book.

The wages book

A wages book is not essential but if you do have one it helps with the overall control of your finances. The basic forms for recording payments and deductions for each employee can be provided by the Inland Revenue upon request. The wages book will contain the same information but will allow you to record the information in a more effective manner. Whether you decide to use a wages book is a matter of choice. It will depend on how many employees you have.

The journal

The journal is used to record all transactions that are not recorded in any of the other books or ledgers. These will, in effect, record the nominal and real accounts and will include the accounts for fixed assets as well as the accounts that are unrelated to actual trading, for example, depreciation.

RECONCILING THE BANK STATEMENT

Each month, as an absolute minimum, you should receive a bank statement. It is extremely important that you check this statement carefully. There could be items such as standing orders or direct debits that have been paid which have been overlooked within your books. By the same token, funds that you have paid in might not have reached your bank account. You must remember that a bank can make a mistake just as easily as you can.

Ticking the items

The very first action to take on receiving the statement is to compare the entries on it to those in your cash book. The simplest way to do this is to tick off the entries that appear correctly in both records, i.e. on the bank statement and in your books.

You can then examine the entries that have not been ticked. These will relate to items that have either been paid from or into the bank account of which you have no knowledge. At this stage remember that credits on the bank statement will relate to debits in your books. Both records are prepared using the same principles but from different perspectives. The money that you have in the account is an asset to you, but a liability to the bank.

Updating the cash book

Once you have identified the missing entries you can update your cash book. It is impractical to try to enter the items on the date that they appear on the bank statement. The practical method is to enter the date as being the date on which you became aware of the items involved.

Although this will bring your cash book up to date there may still be discrepancies between the two records. These will relate to items that are subject to being received or paid by the bank. As examples:

◆ cheques that you have issued that have not yet been presented to the bank for payment

◆ money that you have paid in but which has yet to be credited to your account.

Reconciling the balance

1. To reconcile the position, you start with the new balance in your cash book after it has been updated.
2. To that figure you add back the cheques drawn but not presented.
3. You then deduct the money paid into the account but not yet credited.
4. This should then give you the same figure as the balance brought forward on the bank statement.

If the figures still do not agree then you need to firstly re-check your calculations. The most likely reason for the discrepancy is that you have made a mistake somewhere.

If the problem remains unresolved, see if you can remember an entry for the same amount as the difference. If you do discover that the bank has made an error you should report it to them at once. It does not matter in whose favour the error has been made. You expect the bank to be honest in their dealings with you and they have the same expectation of you.

CONSTRUCTING A TRIAL BALANCE

A trial balance is exactly that, a trial balance. It takes the balances from all of your accounts and ensures that the final total balances. In simple terms, the trial balance consists of two straight columns of figures:

◆ on the left-hand side will be the debit balances
◆ with the credit balances appearing on the right.

Balancing the books

Before you can construct your trial balance you need to first balance off all the various accounts. This will normally be carried out at least once a month. Leaving it any longer than that means that any errors will take you longer to find. Of course, if you have entered each double entry correctly there should not be any errors.

Unfortunately mistakes do happen with, for example, amounts being transposed. This could mean that an item has been entered on one side as £150.67 and on the other side as £160.57. Sometimes these can be very difficult to spot. This is why you must be accurate with all your entries.

> Taking time over entering figures will save a lot of time later in finding any mistakes.

Each time you make the double entry, cross-check it back to the original entry to make sure both are the same.

Phil Stone account					
Date	*Details*	*Amount*	*Date*	*Details*	*Amount*
1.1.xx	Balance B/F	£657.89	7.1.xx	Invoice 7	£261.89
6.1.xx	Invoice 10	£160.88	18.1.xx	Invoice 8	£205.67
15.1.xx	Invoice 11	£98.76	29.1.xx	Invoice 9	£190.33
27.1.xx	Invoice 12	£201.15	1.2.xx	Balance C/F	£460.79
		£1118.68			£1118.68
1.2.xx	Balance B/F	£460.79			

Fig. 2. Example of a balanced account – standard 'T' format.

The example in Figure 2 shows the entries for the month for the sales that have been granted on credit to your customer Phil Stone. On the left are the sales invoices and on the right the record of payments received. At the end of the month the account is balanced and the resultant figure carried forward. Again, note the potential for confusion. You have made sales on credit and therefore the money that is owed to you is an asset of the business. This means that Phil Stone is a debtor in your books.

A sample trial balance
Once you have balanced all of your individual accounts you can then construct your trial balance, which will merely display all the debit and credit totals from all of

the accounts. Hopefully your trial balance, once compiled, will itself balance. Remember:

◆ assets and expenses on the left
◆ liabilities and income on the right.

Figure 3 shows a sample trial balance.

PMC Engineering Trial balance as at 31.12.xx		
Account name	*Debtors*	*Creditors*
Premises	£25,000.00	
Plant and machinery	£15,875.34	
Tools and equipment	£6,543.69	
Capital		£76,549.87
Total debtors	£14,376.23	
Total creditors		£12,890.65
Stock and raw materials	£11,789.12	
Purchases	£67,842.18	
Sales		£134,657.90
Wages and salaries	£42,160.94	
Motor vehicle costs	£8,769.16	
Heat, light and power	£6,798.56	
Cash	£936.00	
Bank	£5,981.65	
Business rates	£1,891.07	
Owner's drawings	£16,134.48	
Totals	£224,098.42	£224,098.42

Fig. 3. A trial balance.

Being aware of errors

The mere fact that your trial balance actually balances does not mean that it is free from errors. There are, in fact, a number of errors that will not be revealed by compiling a trial balance. These include:

- Items that have been totally omitted from your books.

- Items that have been entered in the wrong account.

- Compensating errors where the errors effectively cancel each other out.

- Items that have been entered incorrectly on both sides of the double entry.

- Items that have been entered in complete reverse.

Once again, these demonstrate the requirement of total accuracy when making entries in your books. It is a better use of your time to make the correct entries in the first place, rather than spend time looking for discrepancies later.

THE IMPLICATIONS OF VAT

Value Added Tax (VAT) is a tax that businesses charge when they supply goods and services. It is also charged on some goods and services that are imported into the UK. There are at present three different rates of VAT:

- Standard rate – 17.5%
- Reduced rate – 5%
- Zero rate – 0%.

Standard rate applies for most supplies of goods and services. Reduced rate is payable on supplies of fuel and power used in the home. Zero rate is charged on what could be considered the essentials of life; for example, most food bought for home consumption, books and newspapers and young children's clothing and shoes.

VAT registration

If your business turnover exceeds a certain limit you must register for VAT. The current limit set from 1 April 2003 is £56,000 per annum. There are very strict rules regarding the time limits for registration and if you are in any doubt you should seek the advice of your accountant.

It is also possible to register your business for VAT even if your turnover does not reach the prescribed limit. In this case, registration is done on a voluntary basis. Whether you consider this or not will really depend on your business. In some circumstances, if you will be a net receiver of VAT, i.e. if the VAT that you can reclaim is greater than you collect, it could be to your advantage. The disadvantages, of course, do include the necessity to complete and send in the regular returns. Your books will also be open to inspection by HM Customs and Excise.

Methods of VAT accounting

First there are two flows of VAT, both into and out of the business. The method by which VAT will be accounted for will depend on the size of your business.

- ◆ Output VAT can either be calculated on an invoice basis or on the cash you have actually received.

- ◆ Input VAT can also be calculated on invoices that you have received or on the actual cash you have spent.

In both cases, provided your sales and purchase ledgers have been established correctly, the relevant figures should be easy to calculate. When you originally register for VAT you will receive free guidance and advice on how VAT works from HM Customs and Excise. They will offer you a choice of one or more of the following:

◆ attending a seminar
◆ having a private meeting with someone at your local office
◆ receiving a 'Welcome to VAT' video and leaflet.

Submitting the VAT return

Under normal circumstances you will be required to submit a VAT return every three months. There are circumstances, however, where returns can be submitted monthly or annually. Advice on the requirements for your own business should be sought from your local VAT office.

The VAT return will specify the date by which it has to be returned and, if necessary, the tax due or to be reclaimed. There can be very severe penalties for late or non-payment.

> Make sure you comply with the requirements. It is not advisable to fall foul of HM Customs and Excise.

It is estimated that 50% of businesses that enter insolvency or bankruptcy proceedings do so upon the petition of HM Customs and Excise.

Submitting your VAT Return electronically
Before you can use this service you need to purchase and install a Digital Certificate on your computer. Only

certificates which operate on the Government Gateway can be used, in which respect there are two approved suppliers;

◆ Chambersign
◆ Equifax

Further details on how you can use this scheme and obtain the appropriate Digital Certificate are contained on the HM Customs and Excise website.

KEEPING THE INLAND REVENUE HAPPY

In exactly the same way, you do not want to make enemies with the Inland Revenue. Both they and HM Customs and Excise have sharp teeth that they will not hesitate to use when necessary.

The payment of tax is a legal obligation. Quite apart from your own income tax, if you employ staff you also need to account for their tax. Added to this is also the imposition of National Insurance to consider. Under the Pay As You Earn (PAYE) scheme, the employer deducts the relevant amounts from the employee's earnings and makes payment to the government.

Complying with the regulations

The implications of self assessment have made the subject of tax a very complex issue. This is not an area that I would suggest that you try to deal with yourself. Even if you do consider yourself capable you could be missing out on tax relief that may be available to your business. The allowances change from year to year and you really need specialist advice. If your accountant cannot help in this respect they will be able to recommend a tax specialist that can. Take their advice for their fee could be recouped just from the reductions in tax they may be able to identify.

PAYE

The one area that you may be able to deal with yourself is the PAYE scheme for your employees. As soon as you employ someone you must advise the Inland Revenue. Your local Inland Revenue office will be able to provide you with substantial help and guidance. A number of leaflets are available together with the relevant forms to help you calculate the required PAYE contribution.

The importance of proper accounting

As soon as you start your business you must advise the Inland Revenue. They will then provide you with a leaflet that is full of helpful information on running your business. In addition, they will provide an application form which is then used by both the Inland Revenue and the Department of Social Security to register your business in their books.

In the preface to this book I have outlined the absolute requirement for you to have a proper accounting system. At some stage you may become the subject of an Inland Revenue inspection. This may not be on the basis that you have actually done anything wrong. The Inland Revenue are entitled to make spot checks relating to tax returns.

If you present the inspector with a shoe box full of receipts from which you have compiled your tax return they will not be impressed. This would more than likely lead to a detailed inspection of not only the latest tax return, but also previous tax returns. It would be far better to present your books in good order, with the supporting documentation properly filed away. If you can show the inspector that you are well organised, and perhaps, more importantly, answer their queries straight away, this will place you in a far better light.

Quite apart from impressing the inspector, it will probably be less stressful to you. Order in business is very important. If your business is disorganised it merely shows that perhaps you do not take as much care as you could. As I outlined at the start of this chapter, be accurate in everything you do and life becomes a lot easier.

KEY POINTS

♦ Understand the two simple rules of double entry book-keeping: debit the account of the receiver and credit the account of the giver.

♦ Allocate accounts according to their type: personal, nominal or real.

♦ Make sure that you have some form of documentation for every single entry in your books.

♦ Always double-check each entry that you make in your books to avoid errors – it is better to be accurate first time around than spend time looking for mistakes later.

- Reconcile your bank statement carefully at least once a month and make sure your cash book is correctly updated.

- Balance off your accounts each month and construct your trial balance to ensure that your books actually balance.

- Be aware of the errors that will not be exposed in your trial balance.

- Understand the implications of VAT on your business and seek professional help if you have any questions as to whether you should register or not.

- Advise the Inland Revenue as soon as you start your business and seek their help and guidance on the implementation of PAYE and National Insurance, if you have employees.

$$\left(2 \right)$$

What Are Financial Accounts?

Having explained the basic principles of accounting we can now consider why you do need accounts, together with the components that will be included in those accounts. Financial accounts have evolved over time to meet the current needs of businesses as well as the complex statutory provisions that have been imposed by legislation. As long ago as 1494 an Italian monk named Frater Lucas Pacioli wrote a thesis on the accounting records necessary for the merchant traders of his time.

Keeping financial accounts is the only way in which you can track the flow of funds into and out from your business. This is the most important element for all businesses.

If you have lost control of your cash then you have probably lost control of your business. There is an old adage associated with financial accounts – cash is king. Ignore this at your peril.

WHY YOU NEED ACCOUNTS
Most businesses maintain some sort of accounting record, at the very least using a basic cash accounting

system. Monitoring cash is very important to the day-to-day control of your business, but it will not reveal any profits or losses that you are making.

Come the time for your annual accounts to be prepared, it will be too late to take any action. The trading performance is historic, the losses have been made and you cannot do a thing about it. The losses will have soaked up cash resources and unless you have an extremely good action plan to improve your performance, you are unlikely to be able to gain outside funding.

This is a scenario that is repeated time and time again in all types of businesses. It is not only small firms that fail due to a lack of cash, even large publicly quoted companies have failed for the same reason. If only business owners had taken the initiative and prepared even the most basic of accounts they could have recognised a potential problem before it occurred.

Keeping control of your business

Unfortunately many business owners go out of their way to avoid the preparation of financial accounts. It is difficult to quantify the reasons for this, but the common theme seems to be that they are considered to be irrelevant to maintaining control. This is a grave and fundamental mistake. Control over your finances is a primary business function that you ignore at your peril. As part of that control the accounts that you prepare will be a key indicator as to how your business is performing.

- ◆ The accounts that you compile do not have to meet the exacting standards of the accountancy profession.

- They only need to be used as a tool, as part of your overall management control systems.

- There is absolutely no reason why you cannot compile basic accounts for your own business.

At this point I should make it clear that I am not suggesting you can dispense with the services of an accountant. What I am suggesting to you is that you should use the specialist knowledge of your accountant for expert advice and to finalise your annual accounts. Unless you can afford to pay them for day to day involvement in your business they are of no relevance to the daily financial control of your business.

Statutory obligations
Another good reason for you to maintain adequate accounting records is to comply with legislation. Each year many people fall foul of the Inland Revenue and HM Customs and Excise for failing to keep the proper records. Although, with the exception of a limited company, there is no legislation to force you to keep accounts, you could be in trouble if your business fails and you are declared bankrupt. This applies to any and every business.

- A limited liability company must comply with the provisions of Section 221 of the Companies Act relating to a company's records.

- As a sole trader, or as a partner in a partnership, if you are made bankrupt you could still be charged with failing to keep proper accounting records under section 361 of the Insolvency Act.

The penalties in both cases can be severe. The ultimate sanction for either of these offences is a prison sentence of up to seven years, an unlimited fine, or both.

You should also be aware that these penalties are actually used by the courts. From my own experience as a magistrate I have seen a number of people go to prison for failing to keep proper accounting records.

Limited companies
If you operate as a limited company you are also required to lodge a copy of your accounts at Companies House. Bearing in mind the sensitive nature of accounting information, you will need the assistance of your accountant to ensure that only the very bare essentials are disclosed.

THE DIFFERENT TYPES OF ACCOUNTS
There are four different types of accounts:

◆ projected accounts
◆ management accounts
◆ annual accounts
◆ audited accounts.

Projected accounts
Most business owners have no problem with preparing projections for their business. Most of the high street banks have specialist packs available for businesses that contain specific projection forms for completion. The layout, styling and headings are relatively easy to understand.

The most common form of projected accounting is the cash flow forecast. This deals with the cash requirements of your business, usually over a one-year period. Whilst a cash flow forecast is a valuable management tool it does ignore profitability and its use is therefore limited.

In some cases, a projected balance sheet and profit and loss account are also prepared, but this is usually carried out by an accountant. This is due, in the main, to a lack of understanding by the business owner as to how they should be prepared. In some cases, even after they have been prepared, the entrepreneur is unable to explain exactly what they reveal.

Management accounts

Management accounts are accounts that enable you to manage your business. In most businesses, however, this form of accounts is totally ignored despite their being of the most importance. It is this form of accounts that is of the most value to your business because it is these that will reveal whether you are actually making a profit or trading at a loss.

Management accounts are usually prepared on a monthly basis and are then compared with the projected accounts to assess ongoing performance. The reason, therefore, that these accounts are so important is that they enable you to monitor your performance and to take early corrective action if necessary.

Annual accounts

The third form of accounts are the annual accounts. These will normally be completed as at your year end by your accountant. This form of accounts is just as important to your business, but for different reasons. The annual accounts enable you to take the specialist advice of your accountant; for example, in order to minimise your tax liability.

Your accountant will also ensure that you comply with all relevant legislation concerning your accounting records and returns, especially if you operate as a limited liability company. Depending upon the size and type of your business you may be able to avoid the final type of accounts.

Audited accounts

If you are a limited company with turnover above a defined level then your accounts must be audited by a registered auditor. This means that the auditor will require a greater depth of knowledge of all your transactions. They will check and verify your documentation to make sure that the accounts are correctly prepared.

AN INTRODUCTION TO BALANCE SHEETS

The balance sheet does not fall within the double entry book-keeping system. The reason for this is quite simple. It is a summary, very similar to the trial balance, of all your assets and liabilities. These are, of course, already contained within your individual accounts.

Early convention was that a balance sheet should be compiled with assets on the right and liabilities on the left. Modern methods, however, use a straight line system and this is considered in more detail in Chapter 4.

What will it show?

The balance sheet will show the financial position of your business as at a defined date. It is, therefore, merely a snapshot of your business. The actual figures listed will have fluctuated throughout the year as your business makes sales and purchases. The individual components of the balance sheet will come under three headings:

- assets
- liabilities
- capital.

The first two headings will have a number of sub-headings relating to the individual asset and liability accounts that are in your books. The final heading, capital, will vary depending on what type of business you have. In simple terms at this stage these can be as follows:

- sole trader owner's capital account
- partnership partner's capital accounts (individually itemised)
- limited company share capital.

How is it compiled?

The balance sheet is compiled from the asset and liability figures taken from your trial balance. These figures are placed in a logical format in order to arrive at the net worth, or surplus resources, of your business. In an ideal world, the figure should always be positive. This means that you have a surplus of assets over liabilities and if the business were to fail, you should be able to pay off all of your creditors.

If the figure is negative this means that your liabilities exceed your assets. Without an injection of cash into the business, preferably from your own resources, the business would be unable to meet its debts as they fall due. If you encounter this situation you must seek the immediate advice of your accountant. Even if you operate as a limited company you could still incur personal liability under certain circumstances if you continue to trade.

Is it an accurate value of the business?

The plain and simple answer is 'no'. The balance sheet does not represent an accurate value of the business. You have to remember that the balance sheet is compiled using the 'book' value of assets. For example, if you purchase a motor vehicle the actual cost is entered in the books. Over time this may be reduced by depreciation. This will still not represent the actual resale value of the vehicle should it become necessary to sell it. It could recover more, or less, than the defined 'book' value.

As a further example, consider the accounts of your debtors, the people who owe you money for goods or services that you have provided. When you compile your balance sheet you are making the assumption that all your debtors will meet their obligations. It is possible that some of them may fail to pay their debt. This will, of course, affect the value of your business as well.

Potentially the situation is made worse if your business should actually fail. In this case the value of your assets, especially those such as tools and equipment, plant and machinery, will only be worth what the liquidator can obtain.

Example
As an example, take the decline of the ship building industries in the North East of England whereupon a large amount of machinery was placed up for auction. In some cases, items that were probably worth many thousands of pounds on a 'book' valuation were sold for just a few hundred pounds. At the end of the day they were only worth what people would actually pay for them.

AN EARLY LOOK AT THE PROFIT AND LOSS ACCOUNT
The profit and loss account is probably the most important account for all businesses. Unless you are making a profit there is little point in being in business.

What will it show?
The profit and loss account covers all of your trading activity for the accounting period in question, usually 12 months. This period may vary, however, usually in the first year of trading, not only to take account of the requirements of the Inland Revenue, but also to make your tax return easier to prepare.

◆ The profit and loss account will summarise your sales income, or turnover and itemise the actual cost of those sales.

◆ This will lead to the calculation of your gross profit.

◆ Your other overhead expenses will then be deducted to arrive at a net profit figure.

◆ The profit and loss account will then show how that profit has been distributed using an appropriation account.

Where do the figures come from?

As with all of the other figures in your financial accounts the profit and loss figures will come from your trial balance. The one exception will be the figure for closing stock. The only way that this figure can be accurately gained is by undertaking a physical stock check, or stock-take, of all the unsold goods. A value can then be placed on them, based on the lower of the cost price or the net realisable value. Stock should always be valued on the most conservative basis.

Once you have this information you can then calculate the actual cost of goods sold.

$$\text{Opening stock} + \text{purchases} - \text{closing stock} = \text{cost of goods sold}$$

This method will have given you the relevant information regarding your stock value, but at this stage no double entries have been made in the books. This aspect, together with the actual construction of a profit and loss account, is dealt with in greater detail in Chapter 5 which also provides a specimen of a profit and loss account.

KEY POINTS

♦ Understand that financial accounts are absolutely essential in the control of your business.

♦ Be aware that the lack of adequate accounting records could place you in severe trouble with the Inland Revenue or HM Customs and Excise.

♦ Obtain a business pack from your local bank and

study the financial forecast forms to gain further information on the layout, styling and headings.

- Remember that a balance sheet does not provide a true value of your business.

- You can only check if your business is viable by compiling a profit and loss account.

3

Considering Your Accountant

A word of caution to start with. Anyone can call themselves an accountant or a book-keeper despite the fact that they may hold no professional qualifications whatsoever. For obvious reasons the quality of service that they provide and the business help and advice that they offer, can range widely.

PROFESSIONAL ACCOUNTING CREDENTIALS

We will look at checking an accountant's credentials later in this chapter. The first piece of advice that I can give you, however, is to only deal with an accountant who is a member of one of the professional accounting bodies. The main three in this respect are the Institute of Chartered Accountants, the Association of Chartered Certified Accountants and the Chartered Institute of Management Accountants.

All qualified members of these organisations will have undertaken rigorous examinations before being allowed to use the respective designatory letters of ACA, ACCA, or CIMA. They are all also required to adhere to high professional standards and all of these organisations have established complaint and disciplinary procedures.

In addition, all members of these organisations who prepare or audit accounts are required to have a practising certificate. These are renewable annually provided the accountant complies with the requirements relating to professional indemnity insurance, continuing professional development and the continuity of the practice arrangements outlined by each organisation.

DO YOU REALLY NEED AN ACCOUNTANT?

In plain and simple terms the short answer is yes – you do need an accountant. The true question to be asked is what do you actually need an accountant for? Before you even start your business you need to seek the advice of an accountant.

An accountant can advise you on the correct structure of your business; for example, whether you should operate as a sole trader or as a limited liability company. They can also advise you on the legislation that you may have to comply with; for example, whether you will need to be registered for VAT.

The main point to consider is what exactly you expect your accountant to do for you.

> Many people make the mistake of getting an accountant involved to do something that they should either be doing themselves, or to perform a task that could be done by someone else on a far cheaper basis.

Accountant or book-keeper?

Many businesses refer to their accountant as 'doing the books'. Quite simply, this does not happen. An accountant is not going to waste their valuable time on the mere preparation of basic records. They will employ a clerk in their office to perform this task but they will, of course, charge you accordingly.

A considerable amount of money could be saved by many businesses if they would either keep the basic records themselves, or if they do not have the necessary skills, employ a book-keeper. Hopefully, by the time you finish reading this book, you will have recognised that keeping your own books is not difficult. Even if you still consider that this is not a task for you, it may prompt you to employ a book-keeper so that at least the figures are calculated in-house. It will certainly be cheaper for you in the long run. It will also give you greater control over your financial situation.

Differentiating between an accountant and a book-keeper
An accountant can help you in a number of different ways including:

- complying with legislation
- establishing internal control systems
- assisting with pricing and profitability decisions
- raising finance
- managing the growth of your business.

This is not an exhaustive list. It is intended to give you a focus for the sort of services that can be provided. You will note that I have quite purposely omitted the one service you may have expected – preparing accounts.

The preparation of accounts is your responsibility as the business owner. Legislation requires that proper accounting records be kept and it is you, not your accountant, who will pay the penalty if this is not complied with. If you do not have the necessary skills, or perhaps the time to keep the books, then you need to delegate this task to a book-keeper.

The role of a book-keeper
A book-keeper will not have the specialist skills of an accountant but they should be able to maintain your financial records using the double-entry method. They should also be able to produce a trial balance that can then be used by the accountant to prepare the necessary summary financial statements. This is all part of helping your accountant to help you, which is covered in detail a little later in this chapter.

Help with taxation
This is one area of expertise in which the services of an accountant can prove invaluable. Tax legislation is extremely complex, quite apart from which it changes on a regular annual basis with the Chancellor's Budget. It is also not just income tax that is affected. You have to consider the whole aspect of taxation, from VAT and National Insurance to Self-Assessment or Corporation Tax.

Unfortunately, many businesses do not use the services of an accountant in this respect on the basis of cost. This is a little short-sighted because, with the complexities of the annual tax allowances, it could mean that more tax than necessary is being paid.

> In many cases the fee of the accountant for compiling the tax return could be recouped many times over by the tax savings that may be available.

Even if you do consider that you can deal with this aspect of your business yourself I would strongly recommend that, at the very least, you get your accountant to check your returns before you submit them. I would be very surprised indeed if they could not find an area in which savings can be made.

CHOOSING AN ACCOUNTANT

The choice of accountant is very important. You should see them as being a partner, there to assist you with the running of your business. For this reason, the accountant that you choose needs to be right for you from the very start. This means that you also need to like them on a personal basis. They could be the best accountant available but unless you actually like them you are probably going to be unwilling to accept their advice no matter how good it is.

The other important aspect in choosing an accountant is the question of their fee. It would, for example, be inappropriate for a small business with limited turnover to seek to appoint an accountant from one of the major accountancy practices. The accountant that you choose should be one that is being used by businesses the same size as yours, although they will need to be able to cope with your business as it grows.

The question of what sort of fee is appropriate is very difficult and subjective. It depends on what you expect your accountant to do for you. Only you can assess if the proposed fee represents value for money. There is, of course, nothing to stop you from obtaining comparative quotations from a number of different accountants. Like any market, there is plenty of choice.

Personal recommendations
Obtaining a personal recommendation is one way which can help you make your choice. There are, for example, a large number of business support organisations such as the nationwide network of Business Links which you can turn to for advice. Their advisers will have many links with accountants with whom they can put you in touch.

Some of these Business Links also operate Business Clubs where members can meet on a regular basis, either socially or as part of a business related seminar and these can be useful sources of advice.

You may also have a number of friends who operate their own businesses who can help you in the selection process. Even if this is not the case, you can ask business owners in proximity to you who they use. Most people are quite happy to provide a recommendation if they are pleased with the service received. In many respects this is one of the most important ways in which service businesses gain their clients.

Asking the bank
In the same way bank managers also have contact with a wide range of accountants. They will know the account-

ants that provide a good service and those that do not. If you are also looking to raise finance for your business it is important that your bank manager too has confidence in your accountant.

It is likely that the bank manager will have other customers who operate similar businesses to yours and they will know if any accountant specialises in such businesses. Inevitably, some businesses are more complicated than others and they may require specialist knowledge of particular legislation. If this is the case it is obviously better to appoint an accountant who can offer such knowledge.

CHECKING THEIR CREDENTIALS

Once you have selected an accountant whom you would consider appointing you should telephone them to arrange an appointment. Make sure that you establish that they will make no charge for meeting you on this initial occasion. It is, after all, for their benefit as well as yours and they should be using this meeting as a sales opportunity to gain a new client.

If they insist that a charge will be made, my advice to you would be to strike them off your shortlist. If they want to charge for a meeting such as this they are likely to charge for every minute of their time thereafter. In one of the worst cases I have seen, the accountant has even charged for his time at a social meeting where the client was paying for the lunch!

Look for the right signs

When you first meet your prospective accountant you will soon decide whether you like them or not. You also need to look for a tidy, well organised office. Any signs of disorganisation probably means that the accountant also runs the affairs of their clients on the same basis. Make sure you check that they have a current practising certificate and ask them for references from existing clients. There can be no good reason for them to be unwilling to give details of these to you.

As a final resort and if you are in any doubt as to an accountant's qualifications, all of the three main accounting bodies offer a telephone reference service. By using this service, potential clients can confirm that the proposed accountant is actually a member of that body. If you are thinking of using this service it is, of course, probably better not to appoint the accountant in the first place.

WHAT CAN YOU EXPECT THEM TO DO?

As you will have seen earlier, accountants offer a wide range of services and it is really for you to decide what you want them to do for you. Most accountants are happy to quote for a package of services covering the basic completion of your accounts through to dealing with VAT and other tax returns.

You need to decide what financial accounting you can undertake in-house and weigh this against the costs of using the accountant. As has been stressed previously, the mundane book-keeping tasks are better done in-house with the accountant's expertise only being utilised when it is cost effective.

From the outset of their appointment, the accountant should issue you with a letter of engagement. This should quite clearly set out the tasks that they will perform for you and the fee involved. On a final note, do not consider that the fee quoted is cast in stone.

> As with all service-based businesses, the fee is negotiable depending on the work required.

Basic services

The basic services that the accountant will offer will relate to the general advice and guidance that they can give regarding the initial setting up of your business. This will involve helping you with a choice as to which sort of business – sole trader, partnership, limited partnership, or limited liability company you should operate.

Having reached that decision they should then help you with:

- your financial forecasts
- charting out how your business will be run
- what income you expect to receive
- and what expenses will be incurred.

These will probably also be incorporated into your business plan.

Once you have established your business they can then take your books and records and compile your annual accounts. These will, at the very least, comprise a balance sheet and profit and loss statement. These are covered a little later but, in simple terms, the balance sheet merely contains details of your assets and liabilities and the profit and loss statement contains income and expenditure.

Limited liability companies
If your business has been established as a limited liability company your accountant will also help you with the statutory returns that have to be lodged with Companies House.

Assistance with VAT and PAYE
As part of the service provided you may wish, at least initially, to contract your accountant to deal with your VAT returns and PAYE. On the other hand, they may provide training to allow you to deal with these aspects yourself.

Either way it is a good idea to use the expertise of your accountant. The penalties for late or inaccurate returns to HM Customs and Excise or the Inland Revenue can far outweigh the initial costs of the accountant's involvement. As I have indicated earlier, it is also a good idea to get your accountant to at least run their eye over your tax returns. A penny saved in the cost of the accountant's time could mean a pound more payable in income tax.

Help with designing your accounting system
Most accountants have their own methods of preparing the final accounts on behalf of their clients. Some use computer software and others use paper-based systems. By talking through your own accounting system with

your accountant you can ensure that it will be compatible with theirs. It does not matter whether it is paper-based or on a computer. If you are both using the same system it not only makes life easier for both of you but will also probably reduce the costs payable.

Your accountant should be willing to spend time with you establishing your own system. In some cases accountants offer training facilities to ensure that clients understand exactly what information is required. Remember that keeping proper books and records is a legal requirement.

> The establishment of a good workable system from the outset will make everyone's life a lot easier.

HOW CAN YOU HELP THEM TO HELP YOU?

Unfortunately, some businesses operate a 'shoe box' approach to keeping financial records. They have one box for receipts and one for payments. At the end of the year both boxes are sent to the accountant, together with bank statements, for the accounts to be prepared. Quite frankly this attitude is an accountant's nightmare. They will still complete the accounts but you can expect a hefty fee for their service. With a little bit of thought and a proper accounting system, not only could the accountant's charges probably be reduced, but the accounts themselves would also be completed a lot more quickly.

Keep good records

The prime importance of maintaining good records cannot be stressed strongly enough. An organised, accurate management accounting system will not only be appreciated by your accountant. It will also give you greater day to day control over your business finances. Unfortunately, many business owners do not heed this advice. Some of the more common mistakes, apart from the 'shoe-box' syndrome, include:

◆ Maintaining books that are never balanced or added up until the year-end.

◆ Failing to pass on to the accountant correspondence relating to VAT, PAYE or tax affairs.

◆ Dealing in cash without keeping receipts.

◆ Not filling in cheque book stubs with payee and amount details.

All of these can only serve to irritate your accountant. Unless you help them to help you, it is possible that they could refuse to provide you with a service. Remember, the contract with your accountant is a two-way process. Unless you provide the information in a proper format they may refuse to continue to offer accountancy services.

Separate personal from business records

This is the one mistake that is so common, it is worth mentioning separately. When starting their businesses some business owners do not keep separate records relating to their business. Instead, all payments and receipts are mixed in with their personal finances.

This is very often the case when what started as a hobby or part-time business suddenly takes off to the extent that it provides a full-time opportunity.

> Whatever the size of your business, even if it only makes sales of a few thousand pounds per annum, separate records are a necessity.

It is essential that, at the very least, you open a separate bank account to keep track of your business finances. If you fail to keep separate records, you risk falling foul of the Inland Revenue. Quite apart from which you could be losing out on tax allowances that may in any event fully offset any tax payable.

KEY POINTS

- Seek the services of an accountant before you even start your business.

- Make sure that the accountant you choose is suitably qualified and experienced with your type and style of business.

- Check the accountant's credentials and take up suitable references.

- Decide exactly what services you need from the accountant.

- Make sure you take advantage of any training that they offer to help you keep your accounts.

- Try to make their life easier – help them to help you and you will probably save on their fee.

$$\left(4\right)$$

Compiling Your Balance Sheet

The balance sheet is a financial statement containing details of all your assets and all of your liabilities. It is compiled as at the close of business on a defined day and therefore will only represent the position of your business as at the close of business on that particular day. Because your assets and liabilities will change on a daily basis as you carry on trading, so will the entries in your balance sheet change.

◆ In simple terms, the balance sheet represents all of the things that you own, your assets and then takes away from that figure all of the money that you owe, your liabilities.

◆ The resultant figure provides you with the value of your business, the net worth, or capital stake.

The balance sheet, by its very nature, is not a difficult document to produce. It merely summarises all of the relevant accounts from your double-entry accounting system so as to give you a factual financial description of your business. As with the trial balance, it too must also balance. Even if you have no external liabilities, the business will still owe you the money that you have invested as your capital stake. It will also owe you any profits that have been made. If on the other hand you have made losses, you may owe the business money to cover those losses if they have totally eroded your capital stake.

The balance sheet will show either a solvent or an insolvent business. A solvent business has a positive net worth and an insolvent business has a negative net worth.

FIXED ASSETS

Fixed assets are those assets that are used in the running of the business and they may, or may not, also contribute to profitability.

> Fixed assets remain in the business on an ongoing basis and are all valued at cost price, less any applicable deduction for depreciation.

Virtually all fixed assets will have a limited useful life and therefore their book value is written down on a predetermined basis to try to reflect their actual value in the business. In some cases this can provide a hidden reserve within the accounts, because in some instances the asset is sold for more than its book value at the end of its useful life.

Depreciation is one aspect that you will need to talk through with your accountant because there are a number of different methods by which it is calculated. In addition, there are a number of Statements of Standard

Accounting Practice that will need to be complied with to ensure that they meet accountancy and Inland Revenue requirements.

Land and buildings
These fixed assets are categorised in the balance sheet depending upon the terms on which they are held. For example, land and buildings that are owned on a freehold basis will probably appreciate in value over time and will therefore require regular revaluation. This will ensure that the book value accurately reflects the true value. Once again, this can be a source of a hidden reserve in the accounts, especially if the property has not been valued for some time.

Leasehold property is itemised separately and valued according to the length of the lease. In all cases these are wasting assets, their value diminishing with the length of lease remaining. In some cases, especially with short-term leases, they may be excluded entirely from the balance sheet because of the fact that they have no resale value.

Plant and machinery
These assets will be working assets and probably used to manufacture the goods that are sold. Examples include workshop equipment such as lathes, drilling or milling machines and other such equipment. Some of this equipment could have a long working life and others a shorter one. These items, especially specialised equipment, are notoriously difficult to value on a realistic basis. In a break-up situation it is not unusual for such equipment to be sold at a small percentage of its book value.

Fixtures and fittings

In most cases the balance sheet value of these items will not truly reflect their value. For example, fixtures and fittings could include electric lights or heating radiators. The actual cost will be entered in the balance sheet and depreciated over time but the true value, if they could actually be sold at all, is probably marginally better than scrap value.

Tools and equipment

As the name suggests, these fixed assets relate to the general tools and equipment used in the business. As an example, in a garage business these would relate to any small hand tools used, such as spanners. As with the plant and machinery these can be difficult to value objectively because their resale value is probably minimal.

Vehicles

These can take a variety of different forms. They could relate to heavy wagons and tractor units right down to the car used by the sales director. Valuation of these assets is made easier by the ready second-hand market. In some cases the depreciation method used may cause a hidden reserve. For example, if depreciated over four years to a nil valuation it is likely that the vehicle will actually be worth something in the secondhand market.

CURRENT ASSETS

These are the working assets used within the business. In all cases they are assets that are actually in the form of cash, or assets that can be converted into cash in the normal way of business. For this reason they are also described as liquid assets.

Current assets are therefore part of a trading cycle. Cash is invested into stock which is then sold to a customer who then either becomes a debtor, or who pays cash. In the case of a debtor, when they pay their invoice this creates more cash to be reinvested in stock. In simple terms, the cycle is represented as follows:

Cash → Stock → Sales → Debtors → Cash

Keeping control over your current assets is of prime importance. You must remember that until your debtors actually pay you, the cycle cannot continue in the absence of more cash. This is the downfall of many businesses that have good sales figures but cannot manage to get their debtors to pay on time. This then delays the cycle and in the worst cases can actually lead to business failure.

> You must remember that until you have actually received the cash you have not made any profit.

Stocks

These can take many forms depending upon the type of business that you operate. If you are a manufacturer they may be represented by:

- stocks of raw materials
- work in progress
- stocks of finished goods.

In all cases they represent the value of the stock of goods that you hold, either ready finished or on their way through the production process.

Debtors

This asset relates to money that is owed to you by customers to whom you have sold your goods or services and then allowed them time to pay you. There may also be a separate entry under this heading for prepayments, money that you have paid in advance that is not yet due. One example would be rent paid in advance.

Investments

This type of asset represents investments that you hold in one shape or another. They could be in the form of a long-term deposit with a building society or shares in associated companies or market quoted stocks. The ease with which they can be converted to cash will also differ accordingly. Quoted investments will be relatively easy to convert, although shares in a private limited company could be substantially more difficult.

Cash and bank

These are self-explanatory assets. They represent the cash that is either held within the business offices or in the bank account. Note that these only include credit balances at the bank. If you have a bank overdraft or loan, these are not assets but liabilities. It is money that you owe.

CURRENT LIABILITIES

These represent the debts that you owe that are payable within the next 12 months. It is essential that these are monitored carefully to ensure that sufficient cash is available to meet the liabilities as they fall due. This is one of the major causes of business failure and it usually involves payments due to HM Customs and Excise.

All too often, businesses forget that VAT is not their money. They are effectively acting as unpaid tax collectors for the Treasury. Accordingly, the VAT element of sales is incorporated into cashflow and used to carry on trading.

> In all cases it is essential that the VAT element of sales is put aside ready to accompany the return.

HM Customs and Excise have very little patience regarding unpaid VAT and are one of the most common petitioners of bankruptcy proceedings. Ignore this warning at your peril.

Bank

Liabilities to your bank are usually in the form of an overdraft or loan. Only amounts due within the next 12 months should be included in this figure. The balance of any loan which is payable after more than 12 months will be included later in the balance sheet as a long-term liability.

Creditors

These are usually broken down into sub-headings which might include:

◆ trade creditors
◆ accruals

- preferential creditors
- money due to subsidiary or associate companies.

Trade creditors relate to the money that is owed to your suppliers. Accruals represent debts that are due for payment but which have not yet been paid. As an example, bonus payments due to employees which have been earned although they have yet to be paid. Preferential creditors represent money that is due to the Inland Revenue or HM Customs and Excise. This could be for tax, VAT or National Insurance.

Hire purchase and leasing

These figures represent money that is owed in respect of assets that have been purchased which are being paid for in instalments. In the same way as the bank figure, only the amount due within 12 months should be included, the balance payable after 12 months is a long-term liability.

LONG-TERM LIABILITIES

As you will have already gathered, these are liabilities which are due for payment in excess of one year ahead. In general terms, these will fall into two categories:

- long-term loans
- hire purchase or leasing.

These are not just confined to loans from a bank. It is possible that the directors have invested money into their company on a long-term basis and if there are no fixed repayment arrangements, they may be considered as long-term loans.

CAPITAL

This entry in the balance sheet relates to the owner's stake in the business. It will be shown in a number of different formats depending on the legal status of the business, i.e. a sole trader, a partnership or a limited company. In addition to the capital accounts, there may well be other entries under sub-headings which reflect the reserves of the business which could relate to a revaluation of assets.

The profit and loss account balance is also included under the entry for capital. If profits have been brought forward the figure is added to the capital account and if losses are brought forward these are deducted. The profit and loss account is looked at in more detail in the next chapter.

Limited companies

The capital of a limited company is invested by the shareholders and the type of shares that they hold can vary. The most common are the ordinary shares, the holders of which usually have full voting and other rights. Other types of shareholders could hold, for example, preference shares which may limit their rights to control the running of the company.

Partnerships

The amount invested in the business by each partner is held in their capital account. The capital account usually remains unchanged and represents the partner's long-term investment in the business. Each partner also has a current account which is used for the appropriation of profits and for partner's drawings to be recorded.

Sole traders

The balance sheet of a sole trader is very similar to that of a partnership although the owner's investment in the business and the drawings that are made are usually recorded in their capital account.

CONSTRUCTING YOUR BALANCE SHEET

Having looked at the general components of a balance sheet you can now use this information to construct a balance sheet for your own business. Balance sheets can be in either a horizontal or a vertical format. The important thing to remember is that whichever format you use, it must balance. To ensure that this happens there must always be two entries for every single transaction. For example, when you buy stock your stock value increases and your cash balance decreases.

When making entries in your balance sheet you have only four options for each double entry:

- If you increase an asset you must either decrease another asset or increase a liability.

- If you decrease an asset you must either increase another asset or decrease a liability.

- If you increase a liability you must either decrease another liability or increase an asset.

- If you decrease a liability you must either increase another liability or decrease an asset.

Assuming that as a sole trader this is your first day in business you can construct an opening balance sheet

that will probably look something like the one in
Figure 4.

ASSETS		LIABILITIES	
Cash at bank	£10,000	Owner's capital	£10,000

Fig. 4. Opening balance sheet.

It is possible that you may also be introducing other
assets into your business that you already own; for
example, tools and equipment together with a motor
vehicle. If this is the case, you will need to consult an
accountant to confirm that your valuation of these assets
conforms to both accounting standards and Inland
Revenue requirements.

To start your business you use some of the cash to
purchase from a supplier goods that you propose to sell
on to your own customers in due course. Remembering
the double entry system, your balance sheet will then look
like that in Figure 5.

ASSETS		LIABILITIES	
Stock	£5,000		
Cash at bank	£5,000	Owner's capital	£10,000
Total	£10,000	*Total*	£10,000

Fig. 5. Balance sheet (1).

Using the rules set out above you have increased an asset,
stock, for which you have paid cash, thereby decreasing
another asset. If you had gained the goods on credit,
instead of decreasing cash you would have increased a

liability in the form of trade creditors. This would have produced a balance sheet like the one in Figure 6:

ASSETS		LIABILITIES	
Stock	£5,000	Trade creditors	£5,000
Cash at bank	£10,000	Owner's capital	£10,000
Total	£15,000	*Total*	£15,000

Fig. 6. Balance sheet (2).

Having acquired your opening stock you now sell £2,000 worth of goods for £2,500, split between cash sales of £1,500 and sales on credit of £1,000 which is to be paid for by your customers in 30 days time. Returning to the original format of your balance sheet, where you paid cash for your stock, it will now change to look like Figure 7.

ASSETS		LIABILITIES	
Stock	£3,000		
Debtors	£1,000	Owner's capital	£10,000
Cash at bank	£6,500	Profit and loss	£500
Totals	£10,500		£10,500

Fig. 7. Balance sheet (3).

You can see at this stage that a new entry, profit, has been added to the liabilities side of your balance sheet. Chapter 5 gives a detailed description of how your profit and loss account is constructed. For the time being, however, all expenses related to the business are being ignored. In simple terms, you can see how this figure of £500 has been calculated. You have sold goods for £2,500 that originally cost you £2,000. In practical terms, the double entry for expenses will relate to cash on the asset side and the profit and loss account on the side of liabilities.

Over the next month you purchase further stock to a value of £20,000, only this time your supplier has granted you credit terms. This allows you to pay for £10,000 worth of the goods after 30 days with £10,000 being paid in cash. You sell goods for £25,000 – the cost price being £20,000 – and once again your sales are split as £15,000 in cash and £10,000 being payable by your customers in 30 days. The goods that you previously sold on credit for £1,000 have now been paid for by your customers. You have also invested in a motor vehicle costing £5,000, obtaining hire purchase funding of £4,000 towards the cost. In recognition of your efforts in the business you have paid yourself the sum of £1,000.

All of these transactions will mean the following double entries to your balance sheet:

◆ Stock value increases by £20,000. Trade creditors increase by £10,000 and cash decreases by £10,000.

◆ Sales increase by £25,000, stock decreases by £20,000 and therefore profit increases by £5,000. Cash increases by £15,000 and debtors increase by £10,000.

◆ Debtors decrease by £1,000 and cash increases by £1,000.

◆ Motor vehicles increase by £5,000, with hire purchase increasing by £4,000 and cash decreasing by £1,000.

◆ Your wages reduce profit by £1,000 and cash by £1,000.

Your balance sheet will now look like Figure 8:

ASSETS		LIABILITIES	
Motor vehicle	£5,000	Hire purchase	£4,000
Stock	£3,000	Trade creditors	£10,000
Debtors	£10,000	Owner's capital	£10,000
Cash at bank	£10,500	Profit and loss	£4,500
Totals	£28,500		£28,500

Fig. 8. Balance sheet (4).

If you followed these entries through closely, in working from the previous balance sheet to the one above, you will have noticed that cash at one stage was a negative figure. This was, of course, on the basis that your whole trading for the month was entered in your books in one go. Had the balance sheet been worked on a daily basis, buying and selling stock to meet demand and receiving and paying out cash, this would not have happened.

You will also note that an apparent profit has been made of £4,500 although at this stage this is only a book entry. As yet, you still have cash of £10,000 to collect from your debtors and, until this has been received, your profit is only hypothetical. If, for example, half of your debtors default on payment, your profit of £4,500 will actually turn into a real loss of £500.

Let us now assume that you have been trading for a full year, with sales continuing at virtually the same level as you achieved in your first month. Your balance sheet may now look something like Figure 9.

ASSETS		LIABILITIES	
Motor vehicle	£5,000	Hire purchase	£3,000
Stock	£6,000	Trade creditors	£13,000
Debtors	£15,000	Owner's capital	£10,000
Cash at bank	£20,500	Profit and loss	£20,500
Totals	£46,500		£46,500

Fig. 9. Balance sheet (5).

In order to present this information in a final version of your balance sheet, there are a number of factors to consider. After 12 months the value of the motor vehicle will not be the same as the cost price. You now need to depreciate this asset to reflect its real value in the business. Noting that hire purchase has reduced by 25%, in other words you have contracted to pay for the motor vehicle over four years, it is not unreasonable to depreciate the asset by the same relative amount.

The value of the motor vehicle therefore needs to be depreciated, or written down, by 25% and the cost passed to your profit and loss account. This reduces the value of the vehicle in the balance sheet to £3,750 with the resultant reduction of £1,250 being taken from profits.

You also need to remember that part of the hire purchase debt is a short-term liability, payable within 12 months and the balance is a long-term liability, payable after 12 months time. Only the capital element of the debt is shown in the balance sheet; interest on the debt is dealt with separately in the profit and loss account.

All of this figure information can now be put into a format normally employed by accountants to look like Figure 10.

Fixed assets		
Motor vehicle	£5,000	
less depreciation	£1,250	
		£3,750
Current assets		
Stock	£6,000	
Debtors	£15,000	
Cash at bank	£20,500	
Total current assets	£41,500	
Current liabilities		
Hire purchase	£1,000	
Trade creditors	£13,000	
Total current liabilities	£14,000	
Net current assets (£41,500−£14,000)		£27,500
Long-term liabilities		
Hire purchase	£2,000	
Total net assets (£3,750+£27,500−£2,000)		£29,250
Represented by:		
Capital account	£10,000	
Profit and loss account (£20,500−£1,250)	£19,250	
		£29,250

Fig. 10. Format for figure information.

KEY POINTS

◆ Constructing your own balance sheet is not difficult. Remember to make all entries, one at a time and make sure that the figures still balance after you make any changes.

◆ Think about the changes you are going to make before

Fixed assets		
Land and buildings	£265,000	
Plant and machinery	£57,634	
Fixtures and fittings	£12,768	
Tools and equipment	£34,823	
Motor vehicles	£78,459	
	£448,684	£448,684
Current assets		
Stocks – raw materials	£12,972	
– work in progress	£14,789	
– finished goods	£17,091	
Trade debtors	£34,703	
Prepayments	£2,765	
Investment in associated company	£10,000	
Cash in hand and at bank	£16,998	
	£109,318	
Current liabilities		
Bank loan	£12,000	
Trade creditors	£28,956	
Accruals	£3,150	
Preferential creditors	£6,576	
Hire purchase	£7,620	
	£58,302	
Net current assets		£51,016
Total assets		£499,700
Long-term liabilities		
Bank loan	£108,000	
Hire purchase	£32,750	
	£140,750	£140,750
Net assets		£358,950
Represented by:		
Ordinary shares	£150,000	
Preference shares	£50,000	
Revaluation reserve	£25,000	
Profit and loss account	£133,950	
		£358,950

Fig. 11. Sample balance sheet for a limited company.

you make them and decide which of the four basic options described earlier in this chapter will apply.

- ◆ Always be logical in your approach. Remember that all the entries relate to a transfer of something into, or out of, your business.

- ◆ Seek the advice of your accountant on the depreciation policies that you should adopt.

(5)

Working Through the Profit and Loss Account

Being in business is all about making a profit. Unless you make a profit you will not be in business for very long.

> Only when you make a profit can you hope to invest in your business and expand.

Profits are also the only way in which you can gain a return on your investment in the business. In plain terms, profit is the surplus of income after deducting expenditure.

Unfortunately, the preparation of a profit and loss account is often left to the year end. By this time, however, it is too late to take any action if you have actually sustained a loss. If the profit and loss account had been constructed on a regular basis, for example monthly, it would have enabled you to trim your expenditure or take action to increase your income.

From this you can see that the regular preparation of a profit and loss account is crucial to your ongoing business success. It should be prepared at least monthly with the actual figures compared with your budgeted figures. In this way you can quickly track any variances and then take corrective action to put you back on target.

The profit and loss account will provide you with two key pieces of management information, both of which are equally important:

◆ Firstly you can establish that you are keeping your costs under control and within budget.

◆ Secondly you can ensure that you are reaching, or exceeding, your sales targets.

These are both essential components in tracking your finances and making a profit.

It cannot be stressed enough that profitability is the most important pre-requisite for making a success of your business. You can have a sales turnover running into millions of pounds but unless those sales are made at a profit they are of absolutely no value to you. Think of it in simple terms. If every sale worth £1 costs you £1.10 to make, you are giving away 10p for every sale that you make. How much can you afford to give away before your business fails?

SALES

Sales will take one of two forms:

◆ either paid for in cash at the point of sale

◆ or sales that are granted on credit and which will be paid at an agreed date in the future.

It is important that you are able to distinguish between the two. It is also important to understand that your sales figure may not actually represent the income in terms of cash that has been received.

In both cases you must also ignore the VAT element because whilst this may form part of your income, this money is not yours and therefore should not be included in your sales figures. You must also remember to deduct from your sales figures the value of any goods returned to you by your customers for any reason. It is also necessary to deduct the value of any discounts given to enable you to calculate your true sales figure for the period.

Cash sales

For obvious reasons, cash sales are the easiest to calculate. As soon as you make a sale, cash is received. In terms of your accounting records, however, unless you have a proper control system, cash sales can be the most difficult to establish. This is even more so when a business deals mainly in cash for both sales and purchases.

There is nothing to stop you working in this way but, if you do, it is essential that all payments and receipts are carefully recorded. Many businesses that deal mostly in cash work in this way because it can, at the very least, minimise bank charges. There is little point in paying in cash to the bank account only to draw it out again at the end of the week to pay the wages.

Credit sales

Sales made on credit are a source of confusion to some businesses. Many people consider that because no cash has been received, the sale has not been completed. This is absolutely wrong.

> All credit sales need to be included in the total sales figure for the period in question.

It makes no difference that they have not actually been paid for yet.

The sale is made as soon as the goods are received by the customer with either an accompanying invoice or a separate invoice sent later. The terms of the credit sale, in terms of when an actual payment becomes due, should be clearly established from the outset. Tight control over credit sales should be maintained to ensure that payment is actually received on time. If necessary, a second invoice should be sent as a reminder.

Remember profit

It is essential that you remember that until payment has been received, you have not actually made a profit. A profit figure will be shown in the profit and loss account but that is not represented by cash in the bank account. It will instead be represented by a debtor item in the balance sheet. If that debt turns bad it will be written off in the profit and loss account as a loss against profits.

COST OF SALES

The cost of sales will be the next entry in your profit and loss. This relates to the actual cost of the goods sold which may, or may not, vary with your sales volume. If you operate as a retailer or wholesaler then your cost of goods sold will probably have a direct relationship with the cost of sales. In most cases the figures will be the same.

Note, however, that the cost of goods sold is not the same as the cost of the goods purchased in the same period. There may have been stock brought forward and there will probably be stock still held. Stock valuations are looked at a little later in this chapter.

Production costs

If you operate a manufacturing business then your cost of sales will be calculated in a different way. Quite apart from the costs of the raw materials you are also incurring costs in turning those materials into the finished product. All of these costs need to be included in order to calculate the true costs of sales. In this way you would also need to include the wages of those workers directly involved in the production process.

Direct costs

Direct costs are sometimes also misunderstood. In the manufacturing scenario they are easy to calculate. They are the costs directly linked to production. In other types of business they may, however, be more difficult to identify.

Example
As an example, consider a car repair workshop. The cost of sales does not just include the cost of the parts purchased. It will also include the costs of those staff employed whose time is also effectively sold to the customer.

In this case the cost of sales, apart from the replacement parts, would also include the wages costs of most of the employees. Remember, however, that we are dealing with direct costs. The wages of the office manager, who makes no contribution to sales, would not be included. These will be accounted for later under the overhead costs.

Stock valuations

In order to accurately calculate profits you must have an accurate stock valuation. The simple method of achieving this is to take the stock valuation as at the start of the period, add the cost of stock purchased, then deduct the value of the stock remaining at the close of the period. As an example, at the start of the month you held stock valued at £10,000 and during the month a further amount of stock valued at £40,000 was purchased. At the end of the month stock valued at £12,000 was held.

In this case the stock valuation is calculated as follows:

Opening stock	£10,000
plus purchases	£40,000
	£50,000
less closing stock	£12,000
Cost of goods sold	£38,000

The most important point to remember is that you must value the stock on a cost price basis, i.e. using the actual cost of the goods. You must not calculate stock values based on the selling price. The only exception to this rule is if the stock has a lower resale value than the cost price. This is referred to as 'net realisable value' and could occur if, for example, the stock has been damaged.

Doing a stock check
You must also remember that the only way you can establish the value of both the opening and closing stock is by undertaking a physical stock check. In terms of management figures an estimate of the stock value will suffice but for the annual accounts your accountant will require evidence that all stock has been accounted for.

There are many reasons for this, the most common of which is to establish that no pilfering has occurred. On the other side of the coin, if stock deliveries have not been monitored correctly it is possible that extra stock has been delivered in error. Stock valuations are one of the main areas in which errors are made which directly affect the profit and loss account. Overstating the stock level can reduce the actual sales made and, conversely, understating the stock level can increase the actual sales made. This in turn means that profit is under or overstated respectively.

GROSS PROFIT
Having calculated your sales and the cost of sales for the same period you can now calculate your gross profit, or gross margin as it is sometimes called. Quite simply you take the sales figure and deduct the cost of sales to arrive at your gross profit. You may think that this figure is inconsequential but you should reflect for a moment on a very important aspect of running your business, your break-even point.

Break-even

As the name would suggest, this is the amount of money required for your business to just generate sufficient income to meet all expenditure. In order to generate an actual profit your financial performance must exceed this level of sales. As an example, consider the following scenario:

- Gross profit equates to 20% of sales turnover.
- Overheads amount to £20,000 per annum.

To calculate the break-even figure for this business you need to use the following equation:

$$\frac{\text{Overheads} \times 100}{\text{Gross profit } \%} \qquad \frac{2,000,000}{20}$$

Break-even for this business is therefore achieved with sales of £100,000. Unless this level of sales can be achieved, or the overhead costs reduced, the business will be trading at a loss. As we have already established, trading at a loss for any sustained period of time is likely to mean business failure.

Trading or operating profit

In some circumstances other forms of profitability are calculated after gross profit to take in varying business expenses. For the purposes of compiling your own accounts I would suggest you ignore them. This will mean that you can achieve consistency throughout your records when you make comparisons. This is an important area of management control and is considered in some depth in Chapter 9.

OVERHEADS

Overheads are also sometimes referred to as fixed costs. In essence they are all the other costs of running your business that have not been accounted for elsewhere. Unlike direct costs, which will vary with the level of production or sales, overheads in general are normally fairly constant over time. The important point to remember is that overheads do not contribute to profits. By that I mean the overheads are incurred without having any relationship to sales volumes.

Overheads are the expenses of running the business and relate to payments that are necessary whether sales are made or not.

> It is essential that overheads are kept under tight control.

If you relate back to the break-even point equation above, you can see that any increase in overheads will require a substantially greater increase in sales. In the example given, an increase in overhead of 1% would also bring about the requirement for a 1% increase in sales. In real terms, however, this would equate to additional costs of £200 which would require a further £1,000 in sales to maintain break-even.

Pre-payments

Another important aspect to remember is that, as with all figures in the profit and loss, the overheads must relate to the accounting period in question. As an example, rent is usually paid in advance. If you pay quarterly in advance and are compiling monthly management accounts, the rent overhead will only be one quarter of the payment made. The balancing two-thirds has been paid in advance and is not therefore included in the profit and loss account. The balance pre-paid will be included as an asset and shown accordingly within the balance sheet.

Payments made in arrears

In exactly the same way as pre-payments, some of your overheads will be paid in arrears. In order to accurately compile your profit and loss account you may need to estimate the sums due. Examples of such payments could include your telephone bill, or your heating and lighting costs.

It should be relatively easy to estimate how much is due, in some cases by taking a meter reading and calculating the sum yourself, or in other cases based on past usage. This amount will then be charged to the profit and loss account and then also shown in your balance sheet as a liability. Even though you have not yet received a bill it is still money that is owed by the business to the supplier.

Depreciation

Depreciation is usually the final entry in the profit and loss account prior to the net profit being calculated. Please remember that this entry does not involve the movement of cash into, or out of, the business. It is a charge against profits to correctly reflect the value of the fixed assets within the business.

In general terms there are two main methods of calculating depreciation:

♦ straight-line depreciation
♦ reducing balance depreciation.

Straight-line depreciation
This method depreciates the asset over a set period by the same sum each year. As an example, a vehicle costing £12,500 is estimated to have a useful life of four years with a resale value at that time of £2,500. Using this method the total depreciation of £10,000 would be written off in instalments of £2,500 over each of the following four years.

Reducing balance depreciation
This method of depreciation is sometimes preferred on the basis that a greater sum is written off in the early years and in some cases, this can reflect more accurately the true value of the asset. Using the same example as above, this would provide the amounts of depreciation over the four years shown in Figure 12.

	Depreciation	Depreciation £	Residual value
Year one	25%	£3,125	£9,375
Year two	25%	£2,344	£7,031
Year three	25%	£1,758	£5,273
Year four	25%	£1,318	£3,955

Fig. 12. Example of reducing value depreciation.

Comparing the two results reveals that whilst initially the reducing balance method involves a higher level of depreciation, over time the residual value of the asset increases. This is as opposed to the straight-line method which initially has a higher residual value but ultimately a lower residual balance. As outlined previously, your accountant will advise on the most appropriate method of depreciation to be used in your business.

It is also very important that you check with your accountant whether there are any special depreciation allowances for tax purposes. As an example, to encourage the use of information technology within businesses there is currently a 100% allowance against profits for any qualifying expenditure. This effectively means that you can write off the cost of the asset against profits in the year that it has been purchased rather than spread depreciation over the probable useful life of the asset.

NET PROFIT

Net profit is calculated by deducting the overhead costs from your gross profit. At this stage it also excludes any drawings by the owners of the business, any payments to shareholders in the case of a limited company and taxation. These payments are usually shown at the bottom of the profit and loss account in a separate appropriation account. This aspect is dealt with a little later in this section.

Net profit is obviously of prime importance to you. Even after taking sufficient drawings for yourself there should still be profit left in the profit and loss account to increase the net worth of your business and provide for future investment.

> If you do not make a net profit you will gain nothing from being in business.

This means that you are gaining no reward for the extra effort required to run your own business. In simple terms, you might be better off selling the business, investing the money and finding a job on an equivalent salary. At least that way you will be gaining a return on your investment.

This is something that many small business owners do not appreciate. Whilst the business is providing them with an acceptable income they are happy. Only when they come to retire do they realise that with no retained profits in the business, it cannot be sold to provide them with a sizeable lump sum. Unless they have invested in a private pension, all they are left with is their original investment which, with inflation, is probably now minimal. They are then faced with the prospect of having to carry on working to gain an acceptable income.

Profit allocation

The way in which profits are appropriated, or allocated, will depend on what style of business you operate. In the case of a sole trader the profit is usually passed directly to their capital account from which their drawings for the period are then deducted. It is dealt with in much the same way for a partnership with the profit being allocated to each partner's current account on whatever basis has been agreed.

Limited companies

In the case of a limited company it is dealt with a little differently. The profits of the company belong to the company although the actual amount of profit to be distributed to the shareholders, the actual owners of the company, will be recommended by the directors and decided at the annual general meeting. The distribution of profit is then made to the shareholders by way of dividend. The balance of the profit and loss account is then transferred to reserves.

Figure 13 is not meant to provide you with a definitive list of the headings that you may wish to consider in your profit and loss account. It merely demonstrates the type of headings that are commonly used. Within reason, you are free to use whatever headings will best suit the style and type of your business.

KEY POINTS

♦ Do not include VAT in any of your figures as this money does not belong to your business, it belongs to the government.

♦ Make sure you correctly calculate your cost of sales, it is not the cost of goods purchased. Take extra special care valuing your stock.

♦ Calculate the break-even point for your business and ensure that your gross profit is sufficient to cover your overheads.

♦ Classify your overheads into appropriate headings and then allocate the same expenses to the same headings on a consistent basis.

♦ When constructing your profit and loss account keep it simple, but accurate.

Total sales		£57,481
Opening stock – as at 1 April 200x	£17,534	
plus purchases	£35,667	
Sub total	£53,201	
less closing stock – as at 30 June 200x	£18,275	
		£34,926
Gross profit		£22,555
Less overheads		
Staff wages and National Insurance	£6,600	
Rent and rates	£1,976	
Insurance	£765	
Light, heat and power	£968	
Repairs and renewals	£443	
Motor and travel	£1,893	
Legal and professional	£200	
Accountancy	£150	
Printing, stationery and postage	£548	
Advertising	£760	
Telephone	£186	
Training	£450	
Cleaning	£600	
Bank interest	£12	
Bank charges	£68	
Bad debts	£137	
Depreciation	£960	
		£16,716
Net profit		£5,839

Figure 13. Sample profit and loss account.

(6)

Compiling Forecasted Accounts

Forecast accounts, in cash flow, profit and loss and balance sheet format, are essential to track your business finances. All too often, however, business owners only prepare them when absolutely necessary and usually for the wrong reasons. The prime example in this respect is when they are prepared at the insistence of your bank. This usually means that you are looking to borrow money and if you had prepared them from the outset, you would have seen the need to borrow such money well in advance.

Not having prepared them in advance now places you at a distinct disadvantage. It is more than likely that you have run out of cash and the only way that you can survive is to borrow money. Control of your business has therefore been lost and you are relying on a funder to support you. If you had applied to the funder well in advance, before you actually needed the money, you would have given yourself more options in the event that they should happen to turn your request down.

The only way that you can assess your future finances is by short-term and long-term financial planning. This will cover not just cash, which is of primary importance, but also profitability and growth.

> Cash is like the flow of blood through your veins. If the flow stops you will die. In the same way, if the flow of cash into your business ceases, your business will not survive.

All of the forecasts must be prepared on a realistic basis and if anything you must be pessimistic rather than optimistic. This will, in effect, give you the worst case scenario. It is far better to work on this basis and then demonstrate that you can achieve a better performance.

THE CASH FLOW FORECAST

You will have gathered from what I have said already that this is the most important of all the forecasts. A cash flow forecast is used to project the flow of cash into and out of, your business. It is not concerned with profitability or growth, it is totally focused on your cash situation, normally referred to as 'liquidity'.

Liquidity, in terms of actual cash, is essential to all businesses no matter what their size.

Orders from customers are of no value whatsoever if you do not have the funds to manufacture the goods. In the same way, a warehouse full of stock will not pay the wages unless the goods can be sold and thereby converted into cash.

In simplistic terms cash flows through your business as follows:

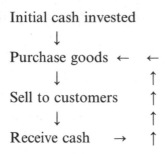

From this simple diagram you can see that if any part of the process is disrupted; for example, late or non-payment by your customers, then you are likely to encounter a shortage of cash. Planning for such disruptions in cash flow will give you greater control over your financial stability and in the long run, the whole viability of your business.

Income from sales

It is extremely important that you accurately estimate the income that you are going to receive. This forms the whole foundation of your business and if you over-estimate the cash you are going to receive you could be placed in serious difficulty. This has, of course, been shown to great effect with the forecasts prepared for the Millennium Dome. So optimistic were the forecasts that within months of opening, with the anticipated visitor numbers not materialising, extra funds had to be obtained to avoid early closure.

Sales income will generally be received either in cash for immediate payment, or on credit for payment at a later date. In terms of completing the forecasts, the cash element can be shown as being received in the month the sales were made. The credit sales will be dealt with differently.

Dealing with credit sales

At the outset you will have agreed a defined payment period for your debtors to pay for the sales that you have allowed on credit. This could be for any term from, say, 30 days up to 90 days, depending on the industry in which you operate.

Once again, however, you need to be pessimistic with your forecasts. Inevitably there will be some slippage in payment receipts and it is better to build them into your forecasts from the outset. In addition, there could be a small element that abuse the credit facility and take much longer than the standard payment time.

It is normal, therefore, to build a further contingency into your forecasts. If, for example, you offer credit terms of 30 days, some forecasts may be prepared on the basis of 70% of sales being received in the month after the sales have been made. A further 20% of the month-one sales will be received in month-three, with the balance of 10% being received in month-four. With experience you will be able to define when payments are actually received and the use of ratio analysis, examined in Chapter 9, will help you in this respect.

Other income

Any other income that you receive which is not related to trading activity will be defined separately in the cash flow forecast. Examples include:

- introduction of new capital
- loans or grants received
- receipts from the sale of fixed assets.

Payment categories

The expenditure that you will incur in business will be broken down into a number of different headings. For example:

- payments to creditors
- salaries and wages
- capital expenditure
- light, heat and power
- rent and rates
- loan repayments.

It does not really matter how many different payment categories you have, the important point is that you remain consistent with your headings. This will make it a lot easier to monitor your expenditure and give you the ability later on to compare your forecasted figures with the actual expenditure. It will also provide you with the ability to make an analysis later of the relationship between different sets of figures; for example, the costs of advertising to the sales generated.

Sample cash flow forecast

Most of the high street banks will have fairly standard cash flow forecast forms and these will help you with the general layout (see Figure 14). Within your cash flow forecast you will also make a number of assumptions and it is important that you set these out clearly. In the cash

	January	February	March	April	May	June	July	August	September	October	November	December	TOTAL
SALES													
Product 1	4000	5500	6500	7500	7500	7600	8500	8500	8000	8000	6500	6500	84,500
Product 2	2000	3500	5500	5500	6500	6500	7000	7000	7000	6500	6500	6000	69,500
Product 3	2000	3500	5000	5000	5000	8000	8000	8000	5000	5000	5000	5000	64,500
TOTAL	8,000	12,500	17,000	18,000	19,000	22,000	23,500	23,500	20,000	19,500	18,000	17,500	218,500
RECEIPTS													
Debtors	4,000	8,250	13,625	16,375	18,250	20,250	22,000	23,125	21,760	20,625	18,875	18,125	205,250
Owners	40000												40,000
Grants	2000			250			250			250			2,750
Loans	30000												30,000
Other													0
VAT	700	1,444	2,384	2,866	3,194	3,544	3,850	4,047	3,806	3,609	3,303	3,172	35,919
TOTAL	76,700	9,694	16,009	19,491	21,444	23,794	26,100	27,172	25,556	24,484	22,178	21,297	313,919
PAYMENTS													
Raw Materials	2800	4375	5950	6300	6950	7700	8225	8225	7000	8825	6300	6125	76,475
Wages & NI	3500	3500	3500	3500	3500	3500	3500	3500	3500	3500	3500	3500	42,000
Rent	1200	1200	1200	1200	1200	1200	1200	1200	1200	1200	1200	1200	14,400
Rates	200	200	200	200	200	200	200	200	200	200	200	200	2,400
Insurance	1650			1650			1650			1650			6,600
HLP	2000			600			600			600			3,800
Telephone	650		350			350			350			350	2,050
Advertising	3500	500	500	500	500	500	500	500	500	500	500	500	9,000
Office costs	465	465	465	465	465	465	465	465	465	465	465	465	5,580
Travel etc	200	200	200	200	200	200	200	200	200	200	200	200	2,400
Professional fees	2500			500			500			500		760	4,760
Repairs	100	100	100	100	100	100	100	100	100	100	100	100	1,200
Other	100	100	100	100	100	100	100	100	100	100	100	100	1,200
Capital	40000			5000			5000			5000			55,000
Bank charges	850			150			150			150		150	1,450
Loan repayments	250	250	250	250	250	250	250	250	250	250	250	250	3,000
Interest	150	150	150	150	150	150	150	150	150	150	150	150	1,800
Drawings	1500	1500	1500	1500	1500	1500	1500	1500	1500	1500	1500	1500	18,000
Tax	9,155	1,171	1,341	2,216	1,569	1,848	2,553	1,845	1,525	2,308	1,508	1,416	28,255
VAT to C & E				(7,139)			4,170			5,780			2,811
TOTAL	70,770	14,811	15,806	16,192	17,484	17,863	29,764	19,335	17,040	29,729	17,073	16,308	282,171
BALANCE	5,930	(5,117)	203	3,298	3,980	5,931	(3,664)	7,837	8,516	(5,244)	5,108	4,991	31,748
BANK BALANCE	5,930	813	1,016	4,314	8,274	14,205	10,542	18,379	26,895	21,651	26,757	31,748	31,748

This cash flow forecast has been prepared by Phil Stone of Parkstone Management Consultancy with information provided by Britannia Engineering.

No responsibility can be accepted for its accuracy.

Fig. 14. Sample cash flow forecast.

flow forecast below the following assumptions have been made:

◆ Sales receipts
   50% in cash
   25% after 30 days
   25% after 60 days.

◆ Bank loan of £30,000 is repayable over ten years with interest fixed at 7.5%.

◆ Grants will be received equating to 5% of capital expenditure.

◆ Raw material costs will equate to 35% of the selling price.

◆ Being a new business no trade credit is available for the first year.

◆ VAT is calculated at 17.5%.

THE PROFIT AND LOSS FORECAST

Once you have completed your cash flow forecasts you can then go to the next stage and construct a forecasted profit and loss account. In many ways it will take the same format as your cash flow forecast. Referring back to Chapter 5 will help you with the suggested layout. In addition, as with the cash flow forecasts, most of the high street banks can provide you with standard forms to set out your forecasted profit and loss account. These are generally referred to as operating budgets.

The operating budget

What you need to remember is that this is a forecast and, as such, it will need to be compiled with monthly figures.

It will not be a summary of your trading position. You must also remember that you are now dealing with profitability and not cash. This will mean that the sales that you make are entered in the actual month in which they occur.

One of the most important points to remember is that profits do not equal cash. We have looked at this point previously but it is worth reiterating. Because of the fact that you are showing credit sales in the month in which they are made you are also attributing the profit on those sales to that month. This, as you will have learnt previously, is not the case. Profit is only received when the actual cash has been received. Up until that time the profit element of the sales is still contained within your debtor figure in the balance sheet.

Linking income to cash flow

For reasons outlined above it is essential that you use the cash flow forecasts and the profit and loss forecasts in conjunction with each other. They cannot be used in isolation to judge the financial performance of the business. Only by meeting your sales targets will you achieve your profitability targets. In the same way, only once you have collected the cash from the sales will those profits be available to be spent. In the interim they are, therefore, both hypothetical figures.

Allocating expenses

The final point that you need to remember when compiling your forecasted profit and loss account is that not all items in the cash flow forecast will be included. You will only include items that are directly related to trading activity. As examples, you will not include within your business income items such as:

◆ capital introduced
◆ loans received.

Likewise, on the expenditure side you will not include such items as:

◆ funds used for the purchase of fixed assets.

The final point to remember when compiling your profit and loss account forecasts is that, unlike the cash flow forecasts, you will also exclude VAT. Although this does relate to funds that flow into and out of your business it has no reflection whatsoever on profitability.

A sample profit and loss forecast is shown in Figure 15. In order to make it actually mean something I have included in Figure 16 the cash flow forecast on which the figures have been based. The figures relating to expenditure have, however, been combined together and are referred to as invoiced items.

THE BALANCE SHEET

The final component of your forecasted accounts is the balance sheet. All too often, however, it is totally ignored. This is a fundamental mistake because you can only identify the individual components of working capital by preparing a forecasted balance sheet.

This means that without such a forecast you cannot identify the following:

- stock levels held
- debtors outstanding
- creditors outstanding.

Without such information you could find that you are running your business without sufficient liquidity. For example, you may be holding too much stock which in turn means that you are using cash unnecessarily. By the same token you may have insufficient money due from debtors to meet your ongoing liability to your creditors. Either of these situations could be distorting your cash flow forecast. Once again, therefore, you need to be looking at the balance sheet forecasts in conjunction with your cash flow and profit and loss forecasts.

New business

With a new business, the opening balance sheet will consist of the assets to be introduced. In some cases this may be as simple as merely showing the cash injected by the owner which is then represented by a cash balance in the bank. This will, of course, also be shown in the cash flow forecasts. In other cases, where fixed assets are to be introduced, these will only appear in the balance sheet. They do not involve any movement of cash.

Once the business starts trading, the balance sheet will then start to reflect the true trading position with the inclusion of the other elements of working capital. Hopefully, over time, it will also include the profit that the business is making.

	Sep 01 £	Oct 01 £	Nov 01 £	Dec 01 £	Jan 02 £
TURNOVER					
Total management sales	47,500	47,500	47,500	20,000	20,000
IT sales	11,878	11,878	11,878	11,878	11,878
	59,378	59,378	59,378	31,878	31,878
DIRECT COSTS					
Purchases	7,601	7,602	7,602	7,602	7,602
Sub contract	641	642	641	642	641
	8,242	8,244	8,243	8,244	8,243
GROSS PROFIT	51,136	51,134	51,135	23,634	23,635
OVERHEADS					
Directors' remuneration	5,226	5,226	5,226	5,226	5,226
Wages & salaries	17,826	17,826	17,826	21,093	21,093
Rent	1,085	1,085	1,085	1,085	1,085
Training	–	3,054	–	–	3,054
Telephone	1,027	1,027	1,027	1,027	1,027
Printing and stationery	469	469	469	469	469
Postage & packaging	159	159	159	159	159
Equipment rental	544	544	544	665	755
Insurance	673	673	673	673	673
Motor expenses	2,260	2,260	2,260	2,260	2,260
Travel and subsistence	1,356	1,356	1,356	1,356	1,356
Advertising	3,164	3,413	3,413	3,413	3,413
Entertainment	212	212	212	212	212
Legal and professional	307	307	307	307	307
General expenses	812	812	812	812	812
Depreciation	94	94	93	94	94
	35,214	38,517	35,462	38,851	41,995
OPERATING PROFIT	15,922	12,617	15,673	(15,217)	(18,360)
INTEREST EXPENSE					
Overdraft interest	724	594	509	353	382
	724	594	509	353	382
NET PROFIT	15,198	12,023	15,164	(15,570)	(18,742)
CUMULATIVE	15,198	27,221	42,385	26,815	8,073

Fig. 15. Sample profit and loss forecast.

Feb 02 £	Mar 02 £	Apr 02 £	May 02 £	Jun 02 £	Jul 02 £	Aug 02 £	Total £
47,500	177,000	–	47,500	70,500	70,500	70,500	666,000
11,878	11,878	11,878	11,878	11,878	11,878	11,878	142,536
59,378	188,878	11,878	59,378	82,378	82,378	82,378	808,536
7,602	7,602	7,602	7,602	7,602	7,602	7,602	91,223
642	641	641	642	641	642	641	7,697
8,244	8,243	8,243	8,244	8,243	8,244	8,243	98,920
51,134	180,635	3,635	51,134	74,135	74,134	74,135	709,616
5,226	5,225	5,226	5,226	5,226	5,226	5,226	62,711
23,892	23,893	23,893	23,893	23,893	23,893	23,893	262,914
1,085	1,085	1,085	1,085	1,085	1,085	1,085	13,020
–	–	3,054	–	–	3,054	–	12,216
1,027	1,027	1,027	1,027	1,027	1,027	1,027	12,324
469	469	469	469	469	469	469	5,628
159	159	159	159	159	159	159	1,908
775	775	775	775	775	775	775	8,477
673	673	673	673	673	673	673	8,076
2,260	2,260	2,260	2,260	2,260	2,260	2,260	27,120
1,356	1,356	1,356	1,356	1,356	1,356	1,356	16,272
3,413	3,413	3,413	3,413	3,413	3,413	3,413	40,707
212	212	212	212	212	212	212	2,544
307	307	307	307	307	307	307	3,684
812	812	812	812	812	812	812	9,744
94	93	94	94	94	93	94	1,125
41,760	41,759	44,815	41,761	41,761	44,814	41,761	488,470
9,374	138,876	(41,180)	9,373	32,374	29,320	32,374	221,146
587	607	132	–	–	–	–	3,888
587	607	132	–	–	–	–	3,888
8,787	138,269	(41,312)	9,373	32,374	29,320	32,374	217,258
16,860	155,129	113,817	123,190	155,564	184,884	217,258	217,258

	Sep 01 £	Oct 01 £	Nov 01 £	Dec 01 £	Jan 02 £
RECEIPTS					
Invoiced sales	69,769	69,769	69,769	69,769	37,457
	69,769	69,769	69,769	69,769	37,457
PAYMENTS					
Invoiced costs	18,663	22,503	29,466	22,796	22,939
Directors remuneration	4,666	4,666	4,666	4,666	4,666
Wages & salaries	15,916	15,916	15,916	18,833	18,833
Overdraft interest	724	594	509	353	382
PAYE/NI	2,210	2,470	2,470	2,470	2,820
VAT	–	19,815	–	–	15,477
	42,179	65,964	53,027	49,118	65,117
NET CASH FLOW	27,590	3,805	16,742	20,651	(27,660)
OPENING BANK	(101,042)	(73,452)	(69,647)	(52,905)	(32,254)
CLOSING BANK	(73,452)	(69,647)	(52,905)	(32,254)	(59,914)

Fig. 16. Cash flow forecast.

Feb 02 £	Mar 02 £	Apr 02 £	May 02 £	Jun 02 £	Jul 02 £	Aug 02 £	Total £
37,457	69,769	221,932	13,957	69,769	96,794	96,794	923,005
37,457	69,769	221,932	13,957	69,769	96,794	96,794	923,005
29,713	23,069	23,068	29,737	23,069	23,068	29,738	297,829
4,666	4,666	4,666	4,666	4,666	4,666	4,666	55,992
21,333	21,333	21,333	21,333	21,333	21,333	21,333	234,745
587	607	132	–	–	–	–	3,888
2,820	3,119	3,119	3,120	3,120	3,120	3,120	33,978
–	–	38,042	–	–	15,900	–	89,234
59,119	52,794	90,360	58,856	52,188	68,087	58,857	715,666
(21,662)	16,975	131,572	(44,899)	17,581	28,707	37,937	207,339
(59,914)	(81,576)	(64,601)	66,971	22,072	39,653	68,360	(101,042)
(81,576)	(64,601)	66,971	22,072	39,653	68,360	106,297	106,297

Existing business

For an existing business the forecasted balance sheets will include opening balances that are based on previous trading performance. These will bring forward the opening balances for all assets and liabilities. As with all of the financial forecasts, the balance sheet for an existing company will be a lot easier to project than that of a new business.

The reasons for this are that some trading history has been established and trends can be used based on previous actual performance. Once again the use of ratio analysis will help with forecasting in this case. This aspect of financial accounts is studied in some depth in Chapter 9.

Sample balance sheet forecast

To help you identify the individual figures, a sample balance sheet appears in Figure 17 based on the forecasted profit and loss and cash flow that are shown in figures 15 and 16.

KEY POINTS

- Forecasted accounts are an essential part of the business planning process. They provide you with clear targets and objectives which can be compared with actual performance to enable corrective action to be taken.

- Always prepare your forecasts on a realistic basis – it is better to exceed them than to have to explain why you have under-performed.

	Opening £	Sep 01 £	Oct 01 £	Nov 01 £	Dec 01 £
FIXED ASSETS					
Fixtures and fittings	6,000	6,000	6,000	6,000	6,000
Accumulated depreciation	(1,500)	(1,594)	(1,688)	(1,781)	(1,875)
	4,500	4,406	4,312	4,219	4,125
CURRENT ASSETS					
Bank	–	–	–	–	–
Trade debtors	55,812	55,812	55,812	55,812	23,500
Other debtors	–	–	–	–	–
	55,812	55,812	55,812	55,812	23,500
CREDITORS DUE WITHIN ONE YEAR					
Bank	101,042	73,452	69,647	52,905	32,254
Trade creditors	18,663	23,710	28,799	23,336	24,686
Other creditors	15,034	22,285	8,884	15,832	18,297
	134,739	119,447	107,330	92,073	75,237
NET CURRENT ASSETS	(78,927)	(63,635)	(51,518)	(36,261)	(51,737)
CREDITORS DUE AFTER ONE YEAR	–	–	–	–	–
TOTAL NET ASSETS	(74,427)	(59,229)	(47,206)	(32,042)	(47,612)
CAPITAL & RESERVES					
Capital	30,000	30,000	30,000	30,000	30,000
Retained earnings	(104,427)	(89,229)	(77,206)	(62,042)	(77,612)
	(74,427)	(59,229)	(47,206)	(32,042)	(47,612)

Fig 17. Balance sheet forecast (continued overleaf).

Jan 02 £	Feb 02 £	Mar 02 £	Apr 02 £	May 02 £	Jun 02 £	Jul 02 £	Aug 02 £
6,000	6,000	6,000	6,000	6,000	6,000	6,000	6,000
(1,969)	(2,063)	(2,156)	(2,250)	(2,344)	(2,438)	(2,531)	(2,625)
4,031	3,937	3,844	3,750	3,656	3,562	3,469	3,375
–	–	–	66,971	22,072	39,653	68,360	106,297
23,500	55,812	207,975	–	55,812	82,837	82,837	82,837
–	–	–	1,939	–	–	–	–
23,500	55,812	207,975	68,910	77,884	122,490	151,197	189,134
59,914	81,576	64,601	–	–	–	–	–
29,586	24,149	25,355	30,150	24,689	25,895	30,691	25,228
4,385	11,591	41,161	3,120	8,088	19,020	13,518	24,450
93,885	117,316	131,117	33,270	32,777	44,915	44,209	49,678
(70,385)	(61,504)	76,858	35,640	45,107	77,575	106,988	139,456
–	–	–	–	–	–	–	–
(66,354)	(57,567)	80,702	39,390	48,763	81,137	110,457	142,831
30,000	30,000	30,000	30,000	30,000	30,000	30,000	30,000
(96,354)	(87,567)	50,702	9,390	18,763	51,137	80,457	112,831
(66,354)	(57,567)	80,702	39,390	48,763	81,137	110,457	142,831

Fig. 17. Continued.

- Income from sales must be accurately assessed – this forms the whole basis of your business and an over estimated figure could lead to business failure.

- Make sure that you account for sales on credit correctly – if anything provide a contingency in your forecasts to deal with those customers who do not pay on time.

- Do not forget to include VAT in your cash flow forecasts and exclude VAT from your profit and loss forecasts.

- Use the forecasted balance sheet to help you plan your liquidity in terms of working capital.

(7)

Working Out the Flow of Funds

Understanding the actual flow of funds through your business is just as important as forecasting as to where it will come from and where it will go. The financial account that you will use in this respect is the source and application of funds statement.

Unfortunately, the formulation of a source and application of funds statement is often considered as unnecessary by many small businesses. It is, however, one of the tools for managing your business and can therefore be used to assist with planning the financial resources of your business.

It provides a link between the opening and closing balance sheets and the profit and loss account for the period. As we have already established, the balance sheet only provides a snapshot of the business as at the opening and closing dates and the profit and loss account relates only to income and expenditure.

THE DIFFERENCE BETWEEN FUNDS AND CASH
We have previously touched on this important aspect, but by using the source and application of funds statement

you can identify the cash and non-cash items. From the outset you must understand the difference between funds, or financial resources and cash.

> Cash is a source of funds, but not all funds are cash. You must understand the distinction so as to ensure that adequate liquid funds are available to finance your business.

Profit is not cash

Just because a business shows a profit in the profit and loss account does not mean that such profit is actually held in cash, although it has funded the business. It is more than likely that the cash generated from sales, including the profit element, has already been reinvested into the business. Such investment may be:

◆ in current assets such as stock which can be used to generate further cash

◆ or fixed assets such as equipment which, of course, will not generate any cash return unless the asset is sold.

In both cases cash has been used to purchase an asset, effectively exchanging one asset for another and accordingly the overall financial resources of the business have not changed. The funds remain in the business but the actual hard cash itself has been utilised. The profit shown in the accounts is therefore merely a book-keeping entry and does not mean that such a sum is sitting in a deposit account somewhere ready to be utilised.

Ignoring depreciation

By the same token, consider the depreciation entry in the profit and loss account. This is an allocation of funds as a charge against profits, although it does not involve any movement of cash. It is merely a book-keeping entry to reduce the value of an asset in the balance sheet so that the amount shown reflects the true value of the asset should it have to be sold to generate cash.

Funding your debtors

The source and application of funds statement will also identify how your debtors are being funded. Remember, debtors are effectively being provided by you with a loan and those funds need to come from somewhere.

Gaining finance from creditors

Funding for your business may also come from other sources that do not involve cash; for example, creditors that allow you time to pay for your supplies. In the same way you may also provide funds to your customers by allowing them time to pay you for goods they have received from you. Neither of these examples would involve any exchange of cash until either your customers pay for the goods or you pay your creditors.

WHAT WILL IT SHOW ME?

In simple terms, the source and application of funds statement:

♦ Shows where financial resources have come from.

♦ Where those funds have been utilised.

◆ Provides a link between the balance sheet and profit and loss account to explain the difference between the financial resources of the business at the start of the accounting period and the end of the accounting period.

There are many different formats for the way in which a source and application of funds statement can be prepared and presented. Two different examples are given later in this chapter. Additionally, it is of course possible for historic or projected figures to be used. Both historic and projected versions would be compiled in exactly the same way, using the same sources for the figure information. Provided you are consistent with the format that you use, it really does not matter how you choose to present the information.

The essential components
There are five essential components of the statement of source and application of funds:

◆ The profit or loss for the period with suitable adjustments for any non-cash items, depreciation being the main example.

◆ Details of any dividends paid.

◆ Acquisitions or disposals of any fixed assets.

◆ Funds raised or repaid relating to external loans or an increase or decrease in share capital.

◆ The increase or decrease in working capital relating to stocks, debtors, creditors and any other current assets or liabilities.

The source and application of funds statement is not a replacement for the profit and loss account and the balance sheet. The information that it contains is a selection, reclassification and summary of the figures contained in those two financial statements. Accordingly, the statement does not indicate the capital requirements of the business and being a snapshot of the financial information, cannot indicate the day-to-day working capital requirements in terms of stocks, debtors or creditors. This information can only be obtained from your cash flow forecast.

Where have I got money from?

It is important that you remember that we are talking about funds and not cash. In this respect it can sometimes be confusing as to where exactly funds have come from. As an example, if your stocks have reduced from the start of the period when compared with the end of the period at which you are looking, this has been a source of funds. In effect the working capital funding requirement has been reduced because stock levels have reduced.

Funds will generally come from one of the following sources:

◆ new capital being introduced
◆ new loans or grants being received
◆ profits – remember to add back depreciation
◆ sale of fixed assets
◆ decrease in stock levels
◆ decrease in outstanding debtors
◆ increase in outstanding creditors.

How have I spent money?

Once again, it is not always clear where funds have been spent. As an example, if your debtors have increased you have effectively given them funding. This has therefore reduced your available funding for other purposes. On the other hand, if you have spent money on the purchase of fixed assets, this can be clearly identified. Funding in the business will generally be applied as follows:

◆ purchase of fixed assets
◆ payments of dividends or drawings
◆ loan repayments
◆ an increase in stock levels
◆ an increase in outstanding debtors
◆ a decrease in outstanding creditors.

WHAT USE CAN I MAKE OF THIS?

The most obvious answer is that it is a further tool to help you control your business. At this stage it is important to remind you that you must retain adequate control over your debtors and creditors to ensure that cash is available, as and when required to fund your business. Allowing your debtors too long to pay you could mean that you run out of cash and your creditors may not allow you to delay payment to them purely because of your lack of control.

Analysing performance

Completing a source and application of funds statement will allow you to analyse and reconcile your financial performance. It will also give you an indication of how much reliance you are placing on the forbearance of your creditors which, under no circumstances, should ever be abused. The statement can also be used in conjunction with ratio analysis which is explained in Chapter 9. This will ensure that either your financial performance is consistent or improving, or will allow you to take steps to rectify the position, if it is deteriorating.

Long-term financial planning

A forecasted source and application of funds statement will help you with the long-term financial planning in your business and enable you to plan your future funding requirements well in advance. The point to always remember is that not all funds need to be borrowed from a bank or other funder. Funding can also, for example, be received by negotiating extended payment terms from your creditors. By the same token, you can gain funds by making collection of payment from your debtors more efficient.

As a further aid to long-term planning you can look at the trends disclosed by your ratio analysis relating to the actual use of funds within the business. This can then be compared with the cash flow forecast prepared previously to aid the formulation of a new cash flow forecast.

> The source and application of funds statement should not be used in isolation. It is only one of the tools available for long-term financial planning.

COMPILING A SOURCE AND APPLICATION OF FUNDS STATEMENT

To compile the statement you need to have both the balance sheet and the profit and loss account. You can only compile the statement using information from both of the other two financial accounts. Using one in isolation will not provide you with sufficient information. For example, the profit and depreciation figures will only be available in the profit and loss account. Likewise, the increase or decrease in stocks, debtors and creditors will only be available in the balance sheet.

The easiest way to understand how the source and application of funds statement is used is to look at an actual example (Figure 20 on page 106). In order to achieve consistency, a profit and loss account and balance sheet are shown first in Figures 18 and 19 on pages 104 and 105 respectively in order to give you an understanding of exactly where all the figures have come from.

As stated previously, there are a number of different formats for a source and application of funds statement, although the example in Figure 20 is the most common. In order to make you aware of the differing styles of presentation another format, which uses exactly the same information but presents it in an entirely different format, is given in Figure 21 on page 107. You should specifically note the different way in which the working capital elements, i.e. stock, debtors, creditors and cash, are treated.

KEY POINTS

◆ Make sure you understand the difference between funds and cash and the different forms that sources and applications of funds can take.

PROFIT AND LOSS ACCOUNT – YEAR ONE

Sales	£218,500	
less direct costs	£54,625	
Gross profit		£163,875
Expenditure		
Wages and NI	£42,000	
Rent	£14,400	
Rates	£2,400	
Insurance	£6,600	
Heating, lighting and power	£3,800	
Telephone	£2,050	
Advertising	£9,000	
Office costs	£5,580	
Travel, etc	£2,400	
Professional fees	£4,750	
Repairs	£1,200	
Other	£1,200	
Bank charges	£1,450	
Depreciation	£11,000	
Total		(£107,830)
Net profit		£56,045
Other income – grant received		£2,750
Interest		(£1,800)
Drawings		(£18,000)
Retained in the business		£38,995

Fig. 18. Sample profit and loss acount.

BALANCE SHEET – YEAR ONE

Fixed assets

Capital equipment	£55,000	
less depreciation	£11,000	
		£44,000

Current assets

Stock	£21,850	
Cash at bank	£31,748	
Debtors	£13,250	
		£66,848

Current liabilities

Loans	£27,000	
VAT	£4,853	
		£31,853
Net current assets		£34,995
Net assets		£78,995

Financed by:

Owner's capital	£40,000	
Profit and loss	£38,995	
Total		£78,995

Fig. 19. Sample balance sheet.

◆ Use the statement to link together your balance sheet, and profit and loss account to aid the analysis of your business's financial performance.

◆ Keep control of your working capital and understand how changes in stock levels and payment terms, for both debtors and creditors, will affect your funding requirement.

Source of funds	
Profit	£54,245
Depreciation added back	£11,000
Funds generated from operations	£65,245
Capital introduced	£40,000
Long-term loan	£30,000
Grants	£2,750
Total source of funds	£137,995
Application of funds	
Purchase of fixed assets	£55,000
Drawings	£18,000
Loan repayments	£3,000
	£76,000
Net flow of funds	£61,995
Working capital	
Stock increase (+) or decrease (−)	**£21,850**
Debtors increase (+) or decrease (−)	**£13,250**
Cash/bank increase (+) or decrease (−)	**£31,748**
Creditors increase (−) or decrease (+)	**−£4,853**
Net increase in funds	£61,995

Fig. 20. Source and application of funds statement, example 1.

◆ Once you have established a format for your source and application of funds statement make sure you keep it consistent to aid future analysis.

Profit	£54,245
Depreciation added back	£11,000
Funds generated from operations	£65,245
Stock increase (−) or decrease (+)	−£21,850
Debtors increase (−) or decrease (+)	−£13,250
Creditors increase (+) or decrease (−)	£4,853
Working capital surplus (+) or deficit (−)	−£ 30,247
True funds generated from operations	£34,998
Capital expenditure (−)	−£55,000
Grants received (+)	£2,750
Drawings (−)	−£18,000
Total funds generated (+) or absorbed (−)	−£35,252
Financed by:	
Capital introduced	£40,000
Loan net increase (+) or decrease (−)	£27,000
Cash increase (−) or decrease (+)	−£31,748
Total source of finance	£35,252

Fig. 21. Source and application of funds statement, example 2.

8

Preparing Management Information

The whole point of management information is to use that information to help you to control your business. Unfortunately, it is a term that most businesses totally misunderstand. They find themselves totally awash with information that either cannot be used or is not used correctly or, worse still, is not used at all. It is essential, therefore, that your management information system be kept as simple as possible.

In this way you can then use the information in a variety of ways to help you control not only your finances but also the whole of your business. Some common uses include:

◆ monitoring of sales and marketing targets
◆ monitoring of costs and expenses
◆ monitoring the efficiency of employees
◆ maintaining tight control over cash flow.

At all costs avoid the maxim of 'paralysis by analysis'. This means in effect, having so much information that you cannot analyse it correctly. Make sure therefore that the information you collect can be easily collated and more importantly, used. There is very little point in gathering information that you cannot use. This is merely a waste of your valuable time.

You need to ask yourself three questions when establishing your management information system:

- What information do I need?
- Why do I need it?
- What will I use the information for?

Unless you can provide a satisfactory answer for all three questions for any piece of information there is probably little value in storing it. At all costs avoid storing information which you 'think I might need in the future'. If you do need something similar in the future you should be able to obtain more up to date information.

WHAT SHOULD BE PREPARED?

Only you can answer this question. It will depend on the size and nature of your business. As an example, a fully computerised stock control system could be essential for the larger retailer but be totally inappropriate for the smaller 'corner shop' retailer.

It really is a question of balance and priorities. As we have seen earlier, a cash-based business will need a good cash accounting system to ensure that all payments and receipts are correctly recorded. On the other hand, this will be of little use to a mail order retailer who receives payment solely by credit card. It is still, in effect, a cash transaction but in the latter case the cash is credited direct to the bank account.

In the same way, for a business that has a sales team that regularly incurs travel expenses it may be more of a priority to issue them with company credit cards. In this way the expenses can be carefully monitored and controlled.

Finding the purpose

As I have already emphasised, a management information system should be there to provide you with information that helps you to control your business. Only information that meets this purpose should be prepared. Every piece of information must have a purpose. If it has no purpose then it has no use.

> At the very least, your management information system must enable you to track your financial performance.

This will enable you to prepare management accounts in the format of profit and loss and balance sheet, which can then be used to compare actual against forecast performance. You will also be able to monitor actual cashflow against your forecasted cashflow. This will give you the ability to take corrective action should your finances not be running as planned.

Setting objectives

As part of your overall strategy for your business you should have set both business and marketing objectives.

These will hopefully have been defined in a way that can be easily measured. In some cases, however, the objectives have been defined in relation to the potential market size and accordingly these can be extremely difficult to measure.

For the purposes of your management information system it is better to have previously quantified your objectives in terms of clear financial terms; for example, an objective to increase sales turnover in the next 12 months by 10%. As a further example, an objective to reduce costs of production down to 30% of sales turnover can also be easily measured. The above objective therefore has two clearly defined points.

It is of course important that whatever objectives you have set for your business, your management information system should be established in such a way that your performance against those objectives can be easily compared.

Working through budgets

Within your management information system you must have the facility to keep track of your budgets. As an example, you may have allocated a certain sum of money to advertising. It is important that you review your spending in such areas to ensure that the budgets are kept under control.

This is one of the key areas in which some businesses fail. Having established tight budgets for expenditure, when the final figures are produced the actual amount spent bears no relationship to the original budget. By maintaining up to date information on what is actually being spent you have greater control over your business.

Keeping cash under control

This is probably the most important area for all businesses. Remember, without cash you cannot survive for very long. Your management information system must enable you to keep control over not only cash but also the other components of working capital that can be turned into cash. This means that you must have effective control over your outstanding debtors and your stocks.

Firstly you will need to establish a clearly defined method for monitoring your debtors. You cannot allow debtors to take advantage of your business and delay payment to you. You should have established clear terms of trade with your debtors from the outset and these need to be adhered to.

Secondly, you need to monitor your ongoing stock levels. Too much stock means less available cash. Too little stock and you risk losing sales. The management information system should enable you to strike a balance and hold just the right amount of stock at any one time.

Making a profit

This has to be the primary reason for you being in business. The need to make a profit is absolute and not negotiable. Without profit you cannot gain a return on your investment.

The management information system must therefore enable you to monitor your ongoing profitability. Hopefully by this stage you will have recognised that this is not a difficult exercise. You should be able to arrange your records in such as way as to facilitate the easy production of management accounts. As stated at the beginning of this chapter, at the very least these need to be in the form of profit and loss account, balance sheet and cash flow.

Ideally these need to be prepared at least monthly. You should have previously prepared your forecasts on a monthly basis and accordingly the actual figures need to be prepared on the same basis.

HOW CAN I MAKE USE OF THIS INFORMATION?

There is an old saying that 'informed managers are better managers'. There is also a saying that 'information is power'. Your management information system should be able to provide you with information that you can use to improve your business. Whilst it is not the intention of this book to discuss a system for recording non-financial information, you should be aware that records should be kept for purposes such as:

- Monitoring competitor activity for new products.
- Maintaining your unique selling point.
- Comparing existing prices in the market.
- Reviewing staff performance.

All of these could be seen as essential elements of the information that you need to run your business. We are, however, concentrating on the financial side of your business and for this reason, only the financial components of your management information system will be considered. In this respect there are two primary uses for the information that you record:

- profitability
- liquidity.

Reviewing ongoing performance

As we have already established you need to be able to constantly assess the ongoing profitability of your business. This means that you must consistently review your performance. You can use the information to make direct comparisons between what you have forecast and what you have actually spent. This aspect is considered a little later in this chapter.

At this stage the review of your performance should be undertaken by collating the figures for the actual money spent under each sub-heading for expenditure that you used previously. This will enable you to compile your management accounts.

Management accounts are, of course, in exactly the same format as your annual accounts although they will only cover a limited period. These can then be used to assess exactly the financial stability of your business and whether you are actually making a profit.

Maintaining liquidity

Earlier in this chapter we looked at keeping cash under control.

> Management information is essential to monitoring your working capital in terms of the non-cash items, i.e. stock and debtors.

You need to use the management information to ensure that your debtors are paying you on time. Any delay could mean a cash shortfall which in turn would mean that you may be unable to pay your own creditors. For this reason you must use the management information system to establish a credit control system. This will involve not only the sending of the original invoice but also the subsequent follow-up action if the debt is not paid within the agreed time.

In terms of stock you can use the management information system to keep stock at its optimum level. You can use the information to track exactly what is being sold and when, and then use that to order replacement stocks. Keeping tight control over stock levels will also help with your management accounts. It will make it far easier to calculate an accurate value of stock levels for use in the compilation of your balance sheet. Always remember, if stock valuations are not correctly calculated this can have a drastic and sometimes adverse impact on your balance sheet.

Appraising capital expenditure
Capital expenditure can involve significant amounts of money and it is therefore important that an appraisal is carried out prior to any investment. Your management information system can help you in this regard provided

you have monitored the performance of your existing equipment.

Examples

You could, for example have a machine that is constantly breaking down and disrupting production. By analysing the costs that you are incurring in this respect in terms of lost production and repairs, you can decide whether it is still cost efficient to continue to maintain or whether it should be replaced.

As another example, if you have a fleet of differing types of motor vehicles it is important that you use the management information system to track the costs of running those vehicles. By keeping statistics on the fuel, maintenance and other charges that you incur for each vehicle, you can quickly establish which type of vehicle is more cost effective. When it comes to replacing any of the vehicles you are now in a better position to make an informed choice as to how they should be replaced.

HOW ACCURATE WILL IT BE?

There can only be one answer – your management information must be absolutely accurate. If it is not accurate then there is little point in compiling it because it could actually mislead you. In the same way, the information must be up to date. Out-of-date information is of little value.

You must remember that management information is exactly that. It is information designed to help you run your business. It is not being prepared for external use, it is being prepared for internal use only. On this basis there is no need to 'massage the figures' to manipulate how they look. By doing this you would only fool yourself.

Building in contingencies

Within your original forecasts you will hopefully have built in a contingency element to your income and expenditure. In essence, you should have allowed for the maximum amount of expenditure and the minimum likely income. By using the figures in your management information system this will, in future, allow you to be far more accurate with your forecasts.

By the same token, it will also record totally unexpected items of expenditure that you did not allow for at all in the forecasts. This will also give you the opportunity to be more accurate with your contingencies and provide for other costs that you did not initially envisage.

MAKING COMPARISONS WITH FORECASTS

To enable you to run your business efficiently you must review your actual trading results against your original forecasts. For many businesses this aspect of running a business is totally ignored. Financial forecasts are put together, the business plan is written and used to raise finance and then the forecasts along with the business plan are put in a drawer and forgotten.

This can only be a recipe for disaster. Unless you carefully monitor your performance on a regular basis using the management information system, you run the risk of running out of cash. Once that happens it can be difficult to raise more finance because all you have demonstrated to the potential funder is that you have failed to keep control of your business.

Relating actual performance to targets

On a monthly basis at least you should take some time to analyse your financial performance for that month. This means that you must categorise and total up all of your income and expenditure and compare the actual figures to your forecasted target figures. Ideally, this should be carried out on a rolling cumulative basis in order that you can compare not only the monthly figures but also the cumulative figures to date.

> Comparing your actual performance against your forecasted figures will enable you to gain a greater understanding of exactly how your business is performing over time.

It may well be that one month's figures could be distorted in some way; for example, a large amount of capital expenditure being deferred for payment one month later than anticipated. This sort of distortion in the figures will have a large effect in both the forecasted month for the expenditure and the actual month in which it was incurred. By comparing the figures on a cumulative basis, however, this type of situation can be evened out.

Taking remedial action

Comparing your figures on a monthly and cumulative basis will also enable you to take corrective action. This does, of course, work both ways. If you are over budget you can trim down future expenditure and if you are within budget, you can either take the savings or spend more in later months. The critical point, however, is that using the management information system does give you a choice.

This is an important point to remember. Maintaining tight control over your finances means that you increase the options available to you. If you constantly monitor your income and expenditure you can adjust your budgets, or your spending throughout the year. On the other hand, if you maintain little or no control over your ongoing finances then you have no options at all. At the end of the year, when the final accounts are prepared, it is too late to do anything if you have made a loss.

KEY POINTS

◆ Keep your management information system as simple as possible – only store data that you will actually use.

◆ Use the management information system to monitor your progress in achieving your objectives.

◆ Keep tight control over your cash and ensure that the management information system enables you to track your liquidity and profitability.

◆ Make sure that the information that you store and the reports that you compile are absolutely up to date and accurate.

◆ Take time each month to review your performance and compare actual figures against budgeted figures.

Analysing Your Performance

Ratio analysis has an important role in business planning but, as with all forms of statistical analysis, there can be many pitfalls in its use. Before attempting to conduct any analysis of your financial performance you must understand how the ratio can be used and also be aware of its limitations.

Ratios in isolation, based on one year's trading performance can mean very little because of the lack of comparable figures. For example, your net profit may equate to 10% of your sales turnover but in isolation the ratio tells you nothing. Is this a good performance or could you do better? Only by comparing this ratio with the same ratio for the next year's trading performance will it actually be of any assistance to you.

> Remember the quotation attributed to Disraeli – 'There are three kinds of lies: lies, damned lies and statistics.'

Financial ratios can be extremely useful but they can also be severely misleading if not used correctly.

UNDERSTANDING RATIO ANALYSIS

Before you even start to use ratios you must understand that they are only an indicator of how your business is operating. However, by themselves they will not guarantee success. Even if you use what may be an industry standard ratio as a yardstick for your own business this does not necessarily mean that your business is operating as it should.

Always remember that a ratio is only an indicator. It is not and never can be, a substitute for good business management. Anyone who tries to run their business by maintaining a certain ratio at a certain level is misusing the whole concept of business ratio analysis.

What are ratios?

A ratio is a means of comparing one figure with another to create a relationship between the figures which, when viewed in isolation, may have little meaning. A ratio is always made up of two parts, a numerator and a denominator, although both of these may involve a combination of figures. This will become evident when later in this chapter we look at some of the common ratios used to analyse financial accounts.

The figures used will need to be relevant to each other to ensure that the end ratio actually has some meaning; for example, profit to sales or assets to liabilities. Making a comparison between figures for, say, your annual profits and your closing bank balance would give you a ratio that has no relevant purpose.

There are also different ways to calculate some ratios. As with all forms of analysis, it sometimes does not matter how you calculate the ratio. The important point is that you remain consistent and use the same comparable figures in exactly the same way. An example of such differences in calculation is given in the later section covering liquidity ratios with the example of stock turnover.

In summary:

◆ A ratio is a figure that is produced from at least two other figures to establish the relationship between them.

◆ By themselves and in isolation they provide little information to you about your financial performance.

◆ They are merely a means of linking together different parts of your financial accounts.

What use are they?
There are two key uses for ratio analysis:

◆ To provide a comparison between two or more variables in your accounts, either as a ratio of one to the other, or expressed as a percentage, or one as a multiple of the other.

◆ To compare the results from two or more sets of financial accounts to disclose the trends and relationships between the figures that would not be evident from the figures alone.

Quite apart from using ratios to assess your own business performance you can also compare your results with other businesses in the same industry or sector. You could, if you were able, obtain the annual accounts of other similar businesses. Alternatively, you could approach organisations such as the Centre for Interfirm Comparison or ICC Business Publications Ltd which provide specialist reports on industry sectors.

The important thing to remember is that ratios merely take two independent parts of your financial accounts to provide a single figure representing the relationship between the constituent components. Only by comparing the same ratios can any trend or pattern be established in your financial performance.

Avoiding the pitfalls

Whilst they are a valuable tool for analysis, ratios are often misused and indeed, often misinterpreted. The first thing that must be stressed therefore is that ratios should be used with caution.

> You must understand the significance of any ratio before the use of ratio analysis will provide any benefit to your business.

The next important point to consider is the relevance of the ratio. The figures being used to calculate the ratio must have some direct relationship with each other. As an example, the ratio calculated using the sales income and advertising expenditure would provide a meaningful ratio. This ratio could be used to allocate future advertising budgets based on forecast levels of turnover.

On the other hand, there would be little point in calculating a ratio based on the expenditure incurred on motor vehicles and telephone costs. Neither of these forms of expenditure have any relationship with each other.

The final pitfall to avoid is that of mixed types of calculations. Most ratios can be calculated in a number of different ways. Always make sure that you are consistent in the way in which you calculate your ratios. Also ensure that if you are making comparisons with ratios contained in specialist publications; for example, ratios being quoted as 'industry standards', that both ratios are calculated in the same way.

USING RATIOS WITHIN YOUR BUSINESS

Using ratios within your business will help you with your future business planning as well as providing an analysis of your past performance. They will enable you to establish the trends within your business both in terms of sales and expenditure.

This can be an important aspect, especially if your business has any element of cyclical trading. This is normally associated with the agricultural industry but it can also have important considerations if, for example, your business is related to the tourism industry. In these sorts of examples the fixed overheads are incurred throughout the year although the actual sales income could be restricted to only a few months of the year.

Reviewing performance

Ratios are very useful for reviewing your financial performance, but this is only once you have an adequate database of figures to actually compare. This does not mean that you have to be trading for more than two years to make comparisons between your final accounts. You can, of course, review your performance using your monthly management accounts.

The only thing you need to consider is that monthly figures can be distorted. For this reason, if you are using monthly figures it is better to average the results rather than take one month's ratio in isolation. For example, if you have calculated your gross profit margin over the last three months as being 20%, 25% and 28%, the average ratio would be approximately 24%.

Setting targets

Ratios are very useful when it comes to setting new targets. If you have carried out a ratio analysis of your historic sales and expenditure you can very easily compile forecast figures based on the ratios that have been revealed. This is one area that most businesses fail to understand.

If, for example, you are presenting forecast information to a potential funder it is important that the figures that you use can be substantiated. In many cases, forecast information is presented which bears no resemblance to historic performance. As an example, if you have previously achieved a gross profit margin of 20%, there is little point in using a margin of 30% in your forecasts unless you can substantiate where the cost savings are to be made.

MAKING COMPARISONS

Quite apart from using ratios to analyse your own performance you can also use them to analyse the performance of other businesses in relation to your own. You do, however, need to exercise caution in this respect to ensure that all ratios are calculated on the same basis. In addition, you need to remember that no two businesses are alike even though they may be in the same market segment.

Industry standards

The possibility of obtaining information on the ratios that normally apply within each industry has already been highlighted earlier in this chapter. Quite apart from exercising caution on the way in which the ratios have been calculated you also need to consider a further dimension.

In the vast majority of cases the ratios have been averaged to obtain the industry standard. This means that a large number of businesses may have been analysed and the results collated. The effect that this can have could be fairly drastic and it is often useful to try to obtain the whole range of figures. For example, the average gross profit margin within any one business sector could be stated as 20%. On this basis the actual range of figures could fall within say 10% and 30% to give the average quoted.

- ◆ Always remember that ratios can be misleading as well as useful.

- ◆ Never, under any circumstances, try to run your own business to meet the industry standard ratios.

♦ Use them instead as part of your business performance analysis to try to improve the running of your business.

Competitor analysis

Ratios can be invaluable for assessing the performance of your competitors, especially if you can obtain copies of their annual accounts. If your competitors operate as limited companies this will be relatively easy as copies have to be filed each year with Companies House. Whilst these filed accounts will not provide full financial information they will, at the very least, enable you to undertake an analysis of their trading performance.

Once again, however, you need to exercise caution. You cannot obtain an effective overview of their performance based on one year's trading performance. You will need to obtain at least two years' sets of accounts although these should, in most cases, contain comparisons of the previous years' performance. In this way you can obtain four years' trading history from just two sets of accounts. As an example, the accounts for the year 2000 will also have the figures for the previous year, 1999. If you then obtain the accounts for 1998 these will also contain the figures for 1997.

EFFICIENCY RATIOS

Efficiency ratios concentrate on your use of funds within the business. They look at the working capital elements within your accounts, i.e. stock, debtors and creditors and establish just how good you are at controlling your finances. There are many different ways that each ratio can be calculated. For example, the sales-to-stock ratio can be expressed in at least three ways:

$$\frac{\textbf{Stock}}{\text{Sales}} = \text{Stock turnover ratio}$$

$$\frac{\textbf{Sales}}{\text{Stock}} = \text{Number of times stock turned over}$$

$$\frac{\textbf{Stock} \times \textbf{365}}{\text{Sales}} = \text{Number of days sales of stock being held}$$

There are other inherent problems because the components are not valued in the same way. The sales figure is the actual selling price of the stock, but the stock contained in the balance sheet is valued at the lower of either cost or net realisable value. Additionally, the stock figure could be inflated or deflated because it only relates to the holding on one day of the year.

The above should demonstrate the importance of your analysis remaining consistent. It does not really matter which calculation method you use. Whilst there are many different ways of calculating the various ratios, in order to avoid confusion only one example of the method of calculation for each ratio will be given.

Stock turnover

In the case of stocks the most common method is the final example above.

$$\frac{\textbf{Stock} \times \textbf{365}}{\text{Sales}} = \text{Number of days sales of stock being held}$$

This reveals approximately the number of days' stock that is being held, which can vary quite widely depending on your business. If, for example, you sell fresh fruit and vegetables your stock holding would probably be no more than a few days. On the other hand, if you run a bookshop you may find that stock turnover, expressed in days, would be substantially longer.

As with all ratios the important aspect is the trend. An increase in the number of days could indicate that you are holding obsolete or damaged items that are ultimately un-saleable. The ideal position is that you only hold that amount of stock considered necessary at any one time.

Debtor receipts

The ratio for debtor receipts should reveal the length of time it takes for your debtors to pay their invoices. This is calculated in the same basic way as the stock ratio:

$$\frac{\textbf{Debtors} \times \textbf{365}}{\text{Sales}} = \text{Time in days it takes for your debtors to pay you}$$

Ideally, the number of days should equate as closely as possible to your terms of trade. The faster you obtain payment the better because this will have a positive impact upon cash flow. If, however, the trend is showing an increase in the number of days this will require investigation for it could be due to some, or all, of the following:

◆ inadequate control over invoicing
◆ slow payment by debtors who are going unchased

- potential bad debts
- market competition forcing an increase in your terms of trade.

Creditor payments

Creditors are calculated using the formula:

$$\frac{\textbf{Creditors} \times \textbf{365}}{\text{Sales}} = \text{Time in days that it takes you to pay your creditors}$$

This ratio will indicate how good you are at paying your creditors on time. It should also be compared to the terms of trade that you have with your suppliers. Any lengthening in the trend, whilst having a positive impact on cash flow, could also indicate problems. It may be that you are having to delay payment to your creditors for exactly that reason, a shortage of cash. This should be investigated, because if you are abusing your credit you could find the facility totally withdrawn with the subsequent and severe impact on your finances.

LIQUIDITY RATIOS

Liquidity ratios examine the relationship between assets and liabilities. They examine the cycle of funds through the business to ensure that stocks and debtors are turned into cash in order to pay creditors.

Current ratio

The first ratio used for this purpose is the current ratio. This is calculated by dividing current assets and current liabilities as follows:

$$\frac{\text{Current assets}}{\text{Current liabilities}}$$

For a healthy business the resultant answer should be at least two. This would indicate that you have twice as many current assets as current liabilities and therefore should be able to meet your debts as they fall due. However, this ratio may distort the true liquid position because it assumes that stocks can be readily converted into cash.

Acid test ratio

The assumption that stock can easily be converted into cash may not be true in practice and therefore a liquidity ratio that excludes stock is also used. Known as the 'acid test ratio' this is calculated as follows:

$$\frac{\text{Cash} + \text{debtors}}{\text{Current liabilities}}$$

The resultant ratio in this case should not be less than one. Anything less would indicate that you could have liquidity problems and be unable to meet your debts as they fall due. It could also indicate that profit margins are being reduced or even that losses are being incurred.

> Out of all of the financial ratios discussed in this book the acid test ratio could be the most important to you in terms of control.

Remember, cash is king. Run out of cash and your business could fail.

Gearing ratio

The next liquidity ratio calculates the relationship between the funds within the business that have been borrowed from outside sources, as opposed to the funds that are invested from internal sources. In simple terms, the debt-to-equity ratio is often referred to as the 'gearing ratio'.

There is often argument about the exact external liabilities to be included in this ratio. Once again, this does not really matter provided you are consistent. It is better to look at the worst case scenario and include all sources of outside borrowing regardless of the term. The equity, or net worth of the business, includes the capital account and retained profits. It is sometimes referred to in the balance sheet as 'surplus resources'. The gearing ratio is therefore calculated as follows:

$$\frac{\textbf{Total borrowing}}{\textbf{Net worth}}$$

It is difficult to give an indication of what constitutes an acceptable gearing ratio. All lenders have their own guidelines which, amongst other factors, depend on the quality of the proposition. In general terms, the amount of borrowed money should not exceed the net worth and therefore the resultant figure should be greater than one.

Working capital ratio

Unfortunately this final liquidity ratio is often ignored, although for an expanding business it can be crucial. In simple terms, the working capital ratio provides an indication of the likely amount of working capital required when sales increase. In order to be clear, working capital is represented by current assets minus current liabilities. The working capital ratio is then calculated as follows:

$$\frac{\text{Working capital} \times 100}{\text{Sales}}$$

The resultant percentage will indicate the additional working capital required for every increase in sales of 100%. For example, if the percentage ratio is calculated as being 25% this would mean that for every £100 increase in sales a further £25 in working capital will be required. Whilst there are many other factors to be taken into consideration when looking at the expansion of a business this ratio does provide at least a rough indication of the effects on working capital.

PROFITABILITY RATIOS

As the name would suggest profitability ratios examine the trend in your profit margins. Profits can be shown in a variety of different stages within your profit and loss account although there are three that are commonly used:

◆ gross profit
◆ net profit before interest and tax
◆ and net profit.

In all cases the ratio is calculated as a percentage.

Gross profit

The gross profit ratio is calculated as follows:

$$\frac{\text{Gross profit} \times 100}{\text{Sales}}$$

The gross profit ratio will vary depending on what sort of business you operate. A manufacturing business could have a high cost overhead, which will mean a higher gross profit margin than perhaps a retailer with a high volume of sales but at a very fine margin.

Any declining trend in the gross profit ratio should be investigated because it indicates one or more of the following:

◆ Margins could be reducing due to competition in the market.

◆ The reduction could be due to increased purchase cost of the goods being sold which cannot be passed on to customers.

◆ The pricing strategy could be inadequate.

Net profit before interest and tax

This ratio is calculated by taking the final net profit figure and adding back the interest and taxation charges that have been levied. In some profit and loss accounts this figure is quoted separately and in others it is necessary to calculate the figure yourself.

Very often this ratio is abbreviated to NPBIT and is calculated as follows:

$$\frac{\text{NPBIT} \times 100}{\text{Sales}}$$

Net profit before interest and tax can also be useful in determining whether the interest being charged can actually be afforded. This is referred to as interest cover and is calculated by dividing the NPBIT by the amount of interest charged. The higher the resultant figure the better. Any figure less than three could indicate potential problems should interest rates rise.

Net profit

As with all the profitability ratios the net profit ratio is calculated as follows:

$$\frac{\text{Net Profit} \times 100}{\text{Sales}}$$

The net profit ratio represents the funds that are being retained in the business to finance future investment and growth. Variations in this ratio are caused by variations in the gross profit margin and the level of overhead expenses. It should show a steady or increasing trend. In the case of a declining trend in the net profit ratio, which is not matched by a similar decline in the gross profit ratio, this will indicate an increasing trend in overhead expenses.

This will require investigation to establish the source of the increased expenditure to enable cost savings to be made for the future. It may also involve a complete review of pricing strategy where expenses cannot be trimmed.

KEY POINTS

◆ Do not use ratios in isolation. Use them to compare performance and establish any trends that may need correction.

◆ Take great care with how you use and interpret ratio analysis – remember they can sometimes mislead if used incorrectly.

◆ When making comparisons with your industry sector ratios or your competitors always ensure that the ratios are calculated in the same way.

◆ Use the efficiency and liquidity ratios to monitor your working capital and cash flow.

◆ Monitor your profitability carefully and investigate immediately when a declining trend is in evidence.

(10)

Using Computerised Accounting Systems

You may think it strange that having spent the last nine chapters explaining how to prepare your own accounts, I should now suggest that you should computerise these accounts. Not at all. You still need to understand what the computer software is doing with your figures and for this reason you need to understand the basic concepts of accounting.

You must remember that the information the computer can provide is only as good as the information you have stored. If you have made fundamental mistakes in entering the data you can only expect to receive inaccurate financial reports.

> You need to take just as much care with a computerised accounting system as you would with a manual financial system.

Using a computerised accounting system will, however, certainly speed up the preparation of your accounts and this can only enhance the way in which you run your business. All businesses, no matter what the size, should be using some form of computer system.

WHY SHOULD YOU CONSIDER COMPUTERISING YOUR RECORDS?

This really is a question that answers itself. Do you really want to organise your records using a paper-based system that will require a substantial amount of work? Whatever business you run, you really should have a full computer system and printer to organise your business. There can be no excuses whatsoever for not having a computer, bearing in mind the substantial reductions in price that have been in evidence over the years. It is no longer necessary to pay thousands of pounds for even the most basic system.

It is not just the financial side of your business that will benefit. You can use a computer to organise all of your correspondence, marketing materials and customer databases, to name just a few functions.

Using technology

The speed of change in the uses of technology has had a drastic effect on all businesses over the past few years. As part of your overall business plan you probably already use up-to-date technology; for example, a mobile telephone and you may indeed already own a computer. The question to ask yourself is whether you are making the most of that technology.

A computer-based accounting system will offer substantial benefits in the way in which you run your business. These will include:

- ◆ less time spent 'doing the books'

- accurate and up-to-date management information
- faster production of annual accounts
- cost savings on book-keeping and accountancy charges.

The use of a computer-based accountancy system will take away the more mundane tasks involved in keeping your own accounts. The point to emphasise at this stage is that your existing records must be kept adequately. If you have an inadequate system now, computerising your accounts will not solve the problem.

Manual versus computer

It must be stressed that a computer-based accounting system is still based on the accounting procedures outlined throughout this book. The financial information is stored in exactly the same way as a paper-based system. The only difference is that the computer makes all the entries for you, based on the information that you enter and it will then prepare the accounts.

This will, of course, make life a lot easier for you. You will no longer have to worry about the accounts actually balancing because each entry that you make is automatically made to both of the relevant accounts or ledgers. All of the transactions do, however, need to be entered accurately. If you make a mistake and enter a figure in the wrong account, for example entering a sale to the wrong customer, the computer will not pick this up. It will, quite happily, make the double-entry.

There are therefore the same potential problems with both a computer-based system and a manual one.

However, if you take the same element of care in making the entries in the first place, the computer system saves you time in the long run.

WHAT SORT OF BENEFITS WILL THIS OFFER?

By this stage you should have recognised the benefits that a computer accounting system will bring. At the very least, it will save you time and hopefully, also money. Anywhere that you can make cost efficient savings in your business should be welcomed.

You may not, for example, need to employ the services of a book-keeper. Instead, you will need a member of staff who can use the software programme. You will no longer need to keep vast amounts of paper-based records. All of your finances can be organised in the computer's memory. With a few simple actions you should be able to gain information on all your customers' accounts, complete with an analysis of their payment records.

> In essence, a computer-based accountancy system will give you greater control.

Management reports

All of the management information discussed in Chapter 8 should be available. Within minutes you should be able to see exactly how your business has performed. This can be analysed on a daily, weekly, monthly, annual or any other time period that you choose. The computer has the information, all you have to do is ask for it.

As examples, the balance sheet and profit and loss accounts are updated with each entry that you make. You can see at a glance how you are doing in terms of the key indicators of profitability and liquidity. You can access these reports at any time you need to and more importantly, take speedy action if your finances are not going as planned.

You could also analyse your debtors and creditors with immediate reports on:

◆ who owes you money
◆ how long they are taking to pay you
◆ who you owe money to
◆ how long their invoices have been outstanding.

All this sort of information is not readily available with a paper-based system. Potentially, it could take you several hours to prepare this sort of analysis with a paper-based accounting system.

Invoicing

You can use a computerised accounting system to look after all of your invoicing for you. This saves duplication because in any event you need to enter all of the sales into your records. All you then need to do is ask the software to produce the relevant invoice.

A computer-generated invoice will also convey an image of professionalism about your business. Apart from that, if the invoice is not paid when it should be, you can automatically produce a follow-up invoice if you choose to. This does of course mean that you must keep the accounting records up-to-date, preferably on a daily basis. If you enter all transactions as they occur you will naturally spend far less of your time on your books.

Payroll

Most accounting software packages either have this facility incorporated into the basic system or available as an 'add on' package. If you do employ staff, this can save you a great deal of time. The reason for this is that the calculation of wages and the production of wage slips is extremely repetitive, especially if your employees are paid exactly the same amount each week.

Quite apart from this, the computer system will keep track of statutory deductions such as Income Tax and National Insurance. When the time comes, the system can also compile the necessary returns and calculate how much is due to be paid.

The only point to remember is that if you use an accounting package to compile your payroll you must keep the core data up to date. Both tax and National Insurance deductions are subject to periodic change by the government and you must make sure that any changes are correspondingly amended within the system. It may well be that in this respect the software provider will provide periodic revisions and this is something that you need to be clear about from the outset.

VAT returns

These returns probably cause the most problems for businesses. If you are registered for VAT you can take away all of the pain and anguish of doing the returns by using a computerised accounting system. The system will control the entire process of calculating VAT and then produce the relevant figures for the return. It will take into account all of your input and output VAT, based on your transactions for the relevant period. This particular part of the software could pay for itself in terms of the time that you would otherwise spend in manually compiling your returns.

As outlined previously you can also now submit your VAT return electronically rather than send a paper return and indeed pay the return electronically. One of the incentives to use this system is that it usually entitles you to an extra seven days to send the return and make payment.

Forecasting

This is another area in which a computer-based accounting system really comes into its own. It will enable you to prepare all of the forecasts and financial statements that we have previously considered, i.e.:

- cash flow forecasts
- operating budgets
- balance sheet
- profit and loss account.

It will be relatively simple for you to base your forecasts on historic performance, quite apart from which you can ask the computer 'what if' type questions. For example, once you have prepared the basic forecasts you could apply a set increase in sales to see what the results would be. On the other hand, you could apply a decrease in sales, or an increase in costs, or both, to see how this would affect your business.

As you will appreciate, these sort of calculations could take you hours to undertake by using a manual system. In addition to the above, you can undertake a detailed analysis of your costs within minutes, comparing any number of combinations of figures using the computer. Once again, these sorts of benefits offer you substantially more control over a paper-based system.

WHAT TYPE OF SOFTWARE SHOULD YOU USE?

There is no easy answer to this question. The best that I can give you is that you should use the type of software that suits you. The choice that you make will depend on a number of factors including:

◆ the type of computer hardware that you have

◆ the size of your business

◆ whether you have, or envisage having, any employees

◆ whether you are, or will be at some stage, registered for VAT.

The real question you need to ask is exactly what is it that you want from the software. You need to decide what functions are essential, what would be nice to have if possible and perhaps even what you do not need at all. The important point to consider is that you will be using this software hopefully for a long time and subject to periodic updates, it must serve its purpose for the foreseeable future.

Making a choice

There are any number of software packages available from a wide number of software houses. Some of the most common are:

◆ Sage.

◆ Quick Books.

◆ Pegasus.

◆ Moneysoft.

I cannot recommend any particular one of these because the choice that you make must be the one that is the most appropriate for your business. Most of these software providers produce a range of software based on the size of the business that will be utilising it. As an example, Sage at present have a number of different accounting packages from the most basic, 'Instant Accounting' up to the most comprehensive, 'Line 100'.

One of the most important considerations you must remember when making your choice is that the software must be capable of growing with your business. Most businesses start out small and then grow over a period of time. It would be pointless purchasing a software solution that did not offer the same facility. Bear in mind that once you have made your choice and entered all of the opening information, you do not want to use that system for a few years only to find that it becomes obsolete and you have to start again.

> When considering your choice make sure that the package allows for upgrades or the addition of further features without you having to enter all of your data again.

You also need to consider a further factor. You may decide that you need to purchase the most complex software solution in order to guard against obsolescence. Nothing wrong with that but, one word of warning, it will also probably be the most difficult to use. It is far better to start with a simple package and then upgrade the software as and when you need to.

Ensuring compatibility with your accountant

This really is part of the decision-making process. Apart from ensuring that the software will follow you as you grow, it is better to purchase software that is compatible with any used by your accountant. There would be little point in purchasing software that could not be used by your accountant also. Without this compatibility you may as well be speaking different languages.

Your accountant can also probably advise you on the most suitable software for your business. They will hopefully already have experience with similar sized businesses to yours and will already have helped others with any problems. You should never be in too much of a hurry to choose your software.

> Make the right decision at the outset and you could well save a lot of time and trouble later.

Timing the transition

This aspect is extremely important if historically you have used a manual accounting system and you are now going to computerise your accounts. You will need to arrange a cut-off date for the manual system after which you will obviously use the new computerised system. This is a process you should not rush. Make sure you understand how your chosen software package works before you attempt to enter any data. A few errors at the outset could well take you a long time to solve later.

You must also make sure that your final manual records balance. The computer cannot later help you solve errors if the initial opening balances were incorrect. You will, for example, need to draw up a final manual balance sheet, and profit and loss account, that will identify and provide the opening balances for the computerised version of your accounts.

The importance of planning

Planning the transition is just as important as actually taking the decision to computerise your accounts and deciding on which software package to use. As with all elements of your accounts, without an accurate and solid foundation you may end up with computerised accounts that themselves can never be accurate.

Getting help

You must be under no illusions. Computerising your accounts is far from an easy process. Many of the business support organisations offer subsidised training in some of the popular computer software packages and wherever possible, you would be advised to gain as much help as you can.

You may also find that the software producers themselves offer specific training in their products, Sage being a prime example. It is well worth checking around before you purchase the software to see what support you can obtain. Do not rely on any help-line offered by the software producer. They are only there to offer technical support. They cannot, and indeed will not, provide free support if you are trying to solve any problems caused by entering data in the wrong place.

> It cannot be emphasised strongly enough that you must know exactly how the software works before you start to use it.

In some cases, especially with a complicated manual-based system, it is well worth enlisting the help of either a professional or the software supplier themselves to manage the transition for you.

KEEPING DUPLICATE RECORDS

This is an aspect that is so often ignored by most businesses with computerised accounts. It can, however, have serious consequences if this task is not undertaken. You cannot ignore the fact that technology does sometimes go wrong and computers are no exception. I have to admit that as an author I am absolutely paranoid about this. All of my books are stored on a computer disk and in many cases, I do not possess a printed version until the book itself is finally published.

If I were to lose the information stored on my computer I would, as a consequence, be absolutely devastated. For this reason, therefore, I have at least three back-up copies stored in different places, including one on a totally remote computer system. This means that if I lose one version due to computer failure I have, in effect, lost nothing. It is merely a minor irritation for me to retrieve a back-up copy.

Making regular copies

From the above you will have hopefully realised that you must make regular copies of your accounting records. At the very least this should be done once a week, although daily would be even better. There are a number of different ways in which you can make copies. You can store a copy in a different place on your hard drive although this in itself is not recommended. If a hard drive fails it usually affects the whole drive and not just segments of it.

A better method would to be use an alternative storage device, for example:

◆ tape drive streamer
◆ zip disk
◆ CD-ROM.

You could also use floppy disks but, once again, for long-term storage personally I would not recommend them. They too can be prone to failure and whilst the information could probably be restored by a specialist, it is extremely expensive. It is far better to spend time and money on an alternative system from the outset and you can then be sure that your records are safe.

Avoiding disaster

The final aspect you must consider for your duplicate records is where to physically store them. You must always bear in mind the threats posed by a break-in to your premises or, even more extreme, the total loss of your business premises through fire. With regards to a burglary, it does not matter whether you have a paper-based accounting system or a computerised one. A thief will probably leave your books behind but he will most likely remove your computer. A fire, of course, will undoubtedly remove both.

Most businesses are advised to store their records in some form of fire resistant cabinet or safe, and for a paper-based system this is probably the best way. It will, however, also be the only way unless full manual duplicate records are maintained, something that is not really feasible for most small businesses. With a computerised accounting system you do, however, have a much safer and inexpensive method at your disposal.

By using one of the alternative storage mediums outlined above it is extremely simple to just remove the tape, disk, or CD and take it away from your business premises with you. In effect, all you need to do is take the item home with you at night and take it back to your business premises the following day.

If you are as paranoid about duplicate records as I am you can, of course, make as many copies as you like and store them in different places. All you need to ensure, as a matter of course, is that all copies are updated regularly. There is little point in keeping any copy that is out-of-date.

KEY POINTS

◆ Before you even consider computerising your accounts you must understand the fundamental elements of basic accounting.

◆ A computerised accounting system can save you time although you must be entirely accurate with every entry – the computer cannot tell if you are posting an entry to the wrong account.

◆ Control over your finances will be greatly enhanced by your ability to obtain instant management reports.

◆ Mundane and time consuming tasks such as payroll and VAT can be handled virtually automatically.

◆ The choice of software you make is important. Do not be in a rush to buy the software and convert your manual accounting system, take time to plan the transition properly.

◆ Always keep duplicate records – preferably at least one copy away from your business premises. Copies cost little to make – the original can take hours, if not days, to restore without an up-to-date copy.

Useful Addresses

Association of Chartered Certified Accountants, 29 Lincoln's Inn Fields, London, WC2A 3EE. Tel: (020) 7242 6855. http://www.acca.org.uk

British Library Business Information Research Service, 25 Southampton Buildings, London WC2A 1AW. Tel: (020) 7412 7457. Fax: (020) 7412 7453.

Business Link Signpost line: (0345) 567 765.

Chambersign Digital Certificates. http://www.chamber sign.co.uk

Centre for Interfirm Comparisons, 32 St Thomas Street, Winchester, Hampshire SO23 9HJ. Tel: (01962) 844144. http://www.cifc.co.uk

Chartered Institute of Management Accountants, 63 Portland Place, London W1N 4AB. Tel: (0207) 917 9256. http://www.cima.org.uk

Equifax Digital Certificates. http://www.equifaxsecure. co.uk/ebusinessid

HM Customs and Excise. http://www.hmce.gov.uk

Inland Revenue. http://www.inlandrevenue.gov.uk

Institute of Chartered Accountants in England and Wales, PO Box 433, Chartered Accountants Hall, Moorgate Place, London EC2P 2BJ. Tel: (020) 7920 8100. http://www.icaew.co.uk

Institute of Chartered Accountants of Scotland, 27 Queen Street, Edinburgh EH2 1LA. Tel: (0131) 225 5673. http://www.icas.org.uk

Key Note Reports, ICC Publications Ltd, Field House, 72 Oldfield Road, Hampton, Middlesex TW12 2HQ. Tel: (020) 8481 8750. Fax: (020) 8783 0049. Website: www.keynote.co.uk

Office for National Statistics, Government Buildings, Cardiff Road, Newport, Gwent NP9 1XG. Tel: (01633) 812973. Fax: (01633) 812599. E-mail library@ons.gov. uk (Economic and business statistics)

UK Official Statistics. http://www.statsbase.gov.uk

Phil Stone, Author and Management Consultant, Parkstone Management Consultancy, 9 Parkstone Close, Hastings Hill, Sunderland, Tyne and Wear, SR4 9PA. E-mail: help@pkstone.co.uk. Website: http:// www.pkstone.co.uk (links to all of the websites above together with a large number of other useful sites can be obtained direct from this site).

Further Reading

Book-keeping and Accounting, Geoffrey Whitehead (Financial Times – Prentice Hall).

Business Accounting – Volume One, Frank Wood and Alan Sangster (Prentice Hall).

Mastering Book-keeping, Peter Marshall (How To Books).

Cash Flows and Budgeting Made Easy, Peter Taylor (How To Books).

Your Own Business, Phil Stone (How To Books).

Index